Relief

Meters		Feet
3050		10 000
1525		5000
610		2000
305		1000
0	Sea Level	0
		Below
152.5		500 Sea Level
1525		5000
3050		10 000
6100		20 000

Scale 1:40 000 000; one inch to 630 miles. Lambert's Azimuthal, Equal Area Projection
Elevations and depressions are given in feet

| | 200 | 400 | 600 | 800 | 1000 | Miles |
| | 400 | 800 | 1200 | 1600 | | Kilometers |

New International Atlas, © Copyright 1989 by
Rand McNally & Company, R.L. 89-S-72

Cosmopolitan World Atlas, © Copyright 1989 by
Rand McNally & Company, R.L. 89-S-72

Enchantment of the World

LAOS

By Judith Diamond

Consultant for Laos: Clark D. Neher, Ph.D., Chairman, Department of Political Science, Northern Illinois University, DeKalb, Illinois

Consultant for Reading: Robert L. Hillerich, Ph.D., Bowling Green State University, Bowling Green, Ohio

CHILDRENS PRESS®
CHICAGO

On a rainy day, a young girl stays dry under a huge banana leaf.

Library of Congress Cataloging-in-Publication Data

Diamond, Judith.
   Laos / by Judith Diamond.
       p.   cm. — (Enchantment of the world)
   Includes index.
   Summary: Discusses the geography, history, people, and culture of the only landlocked country of the Indochinese peninsula.
   ISBN 0-516-02713-1
   1. Laos—Juvenile literature. [1. Laos.]
I. Title. II. Series.
DS555.3.D53   1989   89-34279
959.404—dc20   CIP
                                                   AC

Picture Acknowledgments
AP/Wide World Photos, Inc.: 18, 43, 47, 48 (2 photos), 52, 54, 56, 59, 61, 84
Historical Pictures Service, Chicago: 31, 32
The Image Bank: © Robert Ostrowski: 92 (left), 114 (right)
Journalism Services: © P. Benaich: cover, 9, 10, 11, 19 (left), 22 (right), 44 (2 photos), 103 (top right), 107, 118 (right)
North Wind Picture Archives: 35, 36
PhotoEdit: © Mark Richards: 65 (right), 75
© **Photri:** 12, 15, 16 (2 photos), 19 (right), 66 (left top & bottom), 69 (right), 71, 72 (2 photos), 73, 79 (left), 86, 88, 90, 94, 101, 104, 105, 106, 114 (left)
© **Carl Purcell:** 4, 27, 64 (2 photos), 65 (left), 66 (right top & bottom), 69 (left), 70 (2 photos), 74, 79 (right), 81 (2 photos), 83, 92 (right), 96, 97 (right), 98, 103 (left & bottom right), 111, 118 (left & center)
Root Resources: © Leland LaFrance: 26 (right)
Shostal Associates: 8, 17, 23, 108 (bottom)
The Stock Market: © Bruce Thomas: 5, 6, 22 (left), 24, 39, 108 (top)
Third Coast Stock Source: © Michael Douglas: 82 (2 photos)
UPI/Bettmann Newsphotos: 55, 97 (left), 100 (2 photos)
Valan: © Jeff Foott: 26 (left); © Robert C. Simpson: 28
Len W. Meents: Maps on 15, 18, 23, 24, 27
Courtesy Flag Research Center, Winchester, Massachusetts 01890: Flag on back cover
Cover: Temple in Luang Prabang

A Hmong woman carries water for crops.

TABLE OF CONTENTS

Chapter 1

LAOS—A COUNTRY
IN CHANGE

Laos is a small, landlocked country of only 91,431 square miles (236,804 square kilometers). It is a little smaller than the size of the state of Oregon or the country of West Germany. It is tucked into the mountains of the Indochinese Peninsula in Asia. The northern tip of Laos brushes China and it stretches south toward Cambodia (called Kampuchea from 1975 to 1989). Vietnam lies on the east and Burma and Thailand are on the west. For centuries Laos has been a pathway for invaders, a passage into the lands of its neighbors, and an escape route for the defeated. Legend has Laos beginning in the eighth century as a small mountain kingdom of the adventurer, Khun Borom. From the fourteenth to the sixteenth century, Laos grew until it almost swallowed the Indochinese Peninsula. Now all that is left is a comma-shaped strip curved against the mountains.

LAOS BEFORE 1975

In Laos's valleys along the Mekong River, the Lao Lum communities, who make up one-third to one-half of the

Opposite page: The Mekong River is the main artery of Laos.

Women transplant seedlings in a rice paddy.

population, cultivate shimmering paddies of rice. Farther up in the hills, the Lao Theung farmers, the first settlers of Laos, grow corn and raise livestock. On the mountaintops cling the homes of the Lao Soung, the Hmong, with their fast, mountain-wise horses, their cattle, and their opium.

Prior to the Communist takeover in 1975, Laos's cities were an ever-changing mixture of people shopping, exploring, and conducting business. Chinese merchants bargained with Vietnamese and Indian traders. Young soldiers and Laotian housewives crowded the streets along with newcomers from the rural districts. These people, each with their distinctive dress, might have been from any of the country's over sixty tribal groups. Farther on American Air Force personnel, from the bases where Laotian pilots were trained, consulted with government officials. Buddhist monks in their saffron-yellow robes instructed small boys. Movie theaters displayed colorful, life-size posters of American, Chinese, Thai, or Indian stars. Cars with music blasting

Vientiane, the capital

continually, swept around corners, their loudspeakers blaring.

Vientiane, the administrative center, and Luang Prabang, the old capital, were the major cities of the north. Savannakhet and Pakse were the army and business centers of the south. The country was divided into sixteen provinces with thirty other major towns. Even though 80 percent of the inhabitants were farmers, towns were the market spots and centers of activity.

LAOS AFTER 1975

Now the Americans are gone and, with them, many of the educated professionals. Many of the Chinese merchants have fled as the state took control of their shops. The army officers these days are from the *Pathet Lao*, the Communist rebel movement. The advisers are Vietnamese, not American. Cities are much quieter places. The government has put its emphasis on developing the countryside. There are new buildings in villages and new roads.

Cultivated land in the northern hills

Although there are fewer trained teachers, there are more schools. Literacy for everyone is one of the country's chief goals. No more closely trimmed lawns and flower gardens decorate government buildings. Instead, chicken coops and patches of cucumber, squash, and beans fill the green spaces. Aid from the West left with Western advisers and now every available piece of ground is planted. Vietnamese experts instruct the Laotians about introducing new fertilizers and new ways of agriculture. Ownership of the land has changed. Farmers are expected to cooperate. Sometimes, the government has tried to eliminate private ownership altogether. Many of these new ideas worry the farmers. It is hard to change practices of generations.

THE PHILOSOPHY OF LAOTIANS

Most of the Lowland Lao are Buddhist. Buddha taught that nothing in life is permanent. Humans cannot understand. They make plans and have dreams and desires. But it is all like grasping at a reflection in the water. No matter how humans try, not

When there is work to be done, all family members contribute.

everything turns out as they wish. Sometimes only frustration and unhappiness result. Buddha explains that good people should accept life as it comes. They should be unselfish and uncomplaining, doing good to others in hopes that their next existence will be a little kinder. *Bo pen ngang,* the Laotians say: "There's no problem, if it is going to happen, let it."

Families are very close. Sometimes as many as four generations will live under one roof. Everyone, from the smallest child to the grandmother, contributes. Each person's success and happiness depends on the success and happiness of the family as a whole. Friends and fellow villagers are very important also. Competition is not encouraged. Being first or best means someone else is last.

This is what Laotians are doing now under their new rulers. The people are listening and trying to understand, yet want, as much as possible, to live as they always have. The government, too, is realizing it may have to bend to accomplish its goals.

Chapter 2

MOUNTAINS
AND VALLEYS

THE NORTH OF LAOS

The northernmost provinces of Laos lie wedged between Burma, China, and Vietnam, both separating these nations and connecting them. This area is a region of rugged mountains broken by narrow, V-shaped valleys. Through these jagged peaks and along the fingerlike tributaries of the country's major river, the Mekong, the first migrations of tribal people from Yunnan, southern China, took place. Their descendants are known now as the Lao Lum. As unrest, war, or famine struck, there were other people from homelands north and east of Laos who passed through the same routes. The Mien, the Lu, the Tai Neua, and the Hmong migrated slowly south. Many of these tribes still live in the scattered villages on the mountaintops or along the fertile streams on the valley floors.

It is drier and cooler here among the mountains rising 5,000 to 6,000 feet (1,524 to 1,828 meters). Forty to 60 inches (102 to 152 centimeters) of rain fall each year and temperatures range between 30 degrees Fahrenheit (minus 1.1 degrees Celsius) and 85 degrees Fahrenheit (29.4 degrees Celsius). There are few roads, no

Opposite page: Rugged mountains, broken by valleys, make up the north of Laos.

highways, no railroads, only isolated airstrips and mountain paths. It is the home of Phong Saly Province, and to the east, Sam Neua Province. In these areas Communist guerrillas, called the Pathet Lao, formed their first units—eventually taking control from the Royal Laotian Government. It is here also that the Mekong River enters Laos.

THE MEKONG RIVER

The Mekong River twists and curls among the mountains, branching into a network of smaller streams. The river is the artery of the country, providing water, banks for washing, irrigation, electricity, and transportation. All major Laotian cities are on the Mekong. It journeys southward, increasing in size as it reaches the old royal capital, Luang Prabang.

LUANG PRABANG

From Luang Prabang, in the north, to Savannakhet, about 300 miles (483 kilometers) southeast, is the longest stretch of navigable river in Laos. Possibly for this reason, there has been a city here since the twelfth and thirteenth centuries. Before the Communist takeover in 1975, as far back as anyone can remember, Luang Prabang has been the home of kings and monks. The kings built palaces and rode magnificent elephants in procession. The monks built temples, called *wats*, sacred places of assembly and shrines for statues of Buddha. The buildings are light and airy, glistening with pounded gold leaf and elaborate wooden carvings. Designs within designs intricately trace windows and roofs.

An aerial view of a peninsula in Luang Prabang formed by the crossing of the Mekong and Nam Khan rivers

The newest palace in Luang Prabang was built by the French in the 1800s. It sits in a garden of trees and flowers at the crossing of the Mekong and Nam Khan rivers in the center of the city. It rises up 1,000 feet (305 meters) in front of the palace doors in Phousy, "the hill of colors." Before the king was removed in 1977, soldiers in royal uniforms stood guard or marched in ceremonial display.

Each of the many wats holds its own treasures. The Wat Mai shelters the Buddha known as the Prabang, which gave the city its present name. Laotians honor this Buddha as the nation's protector. It was made in Ceylon in A.D. 874 and is supposed to contain five possessions of the original Buddha in its forehead, chin, chest, and arms. Laotians believe that as long as it is safe, the nation will be safe.

Another temple, the Wat That, has thousands of books in Lao, Thai, and Vietnamese. It is a priceless collection in this country of few libraries.

15

*Buddhist monks (left) and a colorful
market scene in Luang Prabang (above)*

The yellow robes of visiting monks and villagers in their
mountain dress make Luang Prabang one of the most varied cities
in Laos. The mountain people come down to trade or to work a
few months so they can return to their villages with kerosene, salt,
or shoes. Men from the Hmong tribes shape silver bowls and trays
in shops along the side streets. Silver blocks are pounded into
sheets and impressed with traditional designs by hammer and
punch. It is a skill handed down through the generations from
father to son.

Luang Prabang does not only belong to the past. It is the fourth-
largest city in Laos with a population of over twenty-five
thousand. It is one of just four places in Laos where long-distance
calls can be made. Officials take visitors proudly to the large
government fish hatchery and display plans for industry and
hydroelectric power.

Unloading rice that has been transported down the Mekong River

SOUTH ON THE MEKONG RIVER

Back on the river sliding quietly south, the city disappears and the landscape is embroidered with the patterns of rice paddies. Small villages of bamboo houses on stilts circle modest wats. Slowly the boat approaches the province of Sayaboury, and tall forests of pine and teak. Teak with its wood grains of swirling rings is valued for furniture and statues. It is a major export of Laos. The logs are brought to the Mekong by heavy trucks or grunting elephants and floated downstream. The elephants are less common these days, but the province used to be as famous for them as it was for wood. They were trapped to fill the royal stables in Luang Prabang and used to carry kings in ceremonies or soldiers in war.

At the airstrip in Sayaboury city, a plane waits to fly east into Xieng Khouang. In this country of mountains, airplanes have become more important than cars.

The Plain of Jars

THE PLAIN OF JARS

The northern region of Laos is the country's broadest, about 315 miles (510 kilometers) at its widest extent. Phou Bia is tallest among the mountains, touching the clouds at 9,242 feet (2,817 meters). Lesser peaks, home of the Hmong tribes, dot the horizon. Gradually the mountains give way to the rounded hills and broad savanna called the Plain of Jars. This high plateau of grasses and scrubby trees is dotted with more than a hundred large stone jars. They are centuries old. No one knows how or why they came to be here. Some authorities say they were used in burial rites. There is also a legend telling of a Prince Khun Chuang, victorious against the Vietnamese, who had jars of liquor brought to his soldiers in celebration. Six hundred years later they still litter the landscape like so many pop cans from an ancient picnic.

Waterfalls stream down high cliffs (left). As the altitude increases, the land becomes less junglelike (above).

FORESTS

The plain stretches far beyond the jars into what is called a dry monsoonal forest. Forests cover two-thirds of Laos and this is the most common type in the higher, northern regions. Monsoons are wind systems that reverse direction twice a year to separate the seasons into dry and wet. From November to April dry winter air brought by the northwest monsoon blows down from Asia. Then in May the wind changes to bring warm, humid air and rain. In the beginning, the rains come only in the early morning and evening. By July and August, especially in the south of Laos, there may be a constant steamy downpour for a week at a time. High up in Xieng Khouang it is less junglelike. Most trees lose their foliage in the winter leaving the forest stark and bare except for an occasional evergreen. These tall evergreens silhouetted against the

sky give the region its local name of *Moung Pek*: "Pine Mountain."
The undergrowth is dense, sometimes impenetrable, with coarse
grasses and bamboo protecting nests of animals and birds. There
are bears, deer, rabbits, squirrels, partridge, peacocks, pheasants,
and ducks. The rivers and lakes hold carp, catfish, mullet, and
perch; while on the grassland of the plains, wild buffalo and ox
feed.

THE ANNAMITE MOUNTAIN CHAIN

As the Mekong River separates Laos on the west from Thailand
and Burma, so the Annamite Mountain chain on the east divides
Laos and Vietnam. Rising at the edge of the Plain of Jars, the
mountains formed the passageways of the famous Ho Chi Minh
Trail. During the years of war between North and South Vietnam,
especially in the 1960s and 1970s, these supply routes threaded
through the mountainsides. At first they were only trails, slices of
Laos borrowed for the war. Men in single file carrying packs on
their heads or backs beside small, heavily ladened horses made
their way over the rocks. Laos, small and weak and with
Communists of its own, was powerless to stop them. What started
slowly became a constant stream of soldiers and arms. The world
named the rocky strips the Ho Chi Minh Trail after the president
of North Vietnam. Eventually, the paths were made into roads for
trucks. The armies of South Vietnam and the United States sent
their planes to bomb the trails in order to stop the movement of
weapons and supplies to the Communists in South Vietnam. By
1973 close to two million tons of bombs had been dropped on
Laos, primarily on the Ho Chi Minh Trail. This equaled all the
bombs dropped on Europe and the Pacific during World War II.

However only 15 to 20 percent of all the materials going down the trails were destroyed. A bomb would fall, men would scatter into the forest, and then return to continue their journey.

Today the Ho Chi Minh Trail is the Ho Chi Minh Road. Laos and Vietnam are allies. The war is over. The road is crowded with cars and trucks carrying trade goods, buinessmen, and officials from the north of Vietnam to the south. The highway's violent past is left only as a memory.

VIENTIANE, THE CAPITAL

From Xieng Khouang and the mountains of the northeast, it is only a few hours by air back to the administrative capital, Vientiane. But it is a journey from mountain villages and a life-style that has existed for hundreds of years to a city in contact with the modern world. Vientiane has been attacked, destroyed, and reconstructed many times. Thai armies leveled the city in 1829. It was not rebuilt again until 1860 when the French unified Laos and chose it as the capital. The streets stretch out from the Memorial to the Dead like a star. Lan Xang Avenue is the broadest. It used to be lined with trees, especially the champac tree with its slender, dark-green leaves and pale-yellow flowers hanging in sweet, fragrant strings. The streets have been broadened now, and except for a scattering of mahogany, the trees are gone. But they still stand in the parks and behind the houses filling the evening air with their scent. One of the most famous Laotian folk dances is dedicated to the beauty of the champac tree.

In the marketplace, the stalls are full. Since there are very few refrigerators, most people shop every day. One stand may have bamboo baskets of fresh fish, another flowers and produce, such

Fresh produce for sale in the marketplace in Vientiane (left);
The Memorial to the Dead (right) commemorates the country's veterans.

as melons, cucumbers, beans, and dried mushrooms. Not only food, but tools, knives, and pots and pans as well as clothes are displayed for the crowds of shoppers. Blue jeans from Thailand are especially popular. There are children's books too and old copies of the Soviet newspaper, *Pravda*. Each day the Lao government publishes its own newspaper, *Pasason* (*The People*) with four pages of editorials, provincial news, youth columns, and moral lessons.

The most important buildings are governmental: the Treasury, the National Assembly, the courts, and the university. They are low and graceful, gleaming white in the sun.

At the edge of the city is a suburb known as Kilometer 6. It was built in the 1960s by American and European technical experts who wanted a small corner of the West in Laos. Now, however, the rows of ranch-style houses hold Vietnamese, Soviet, and

Vientiane

Annamite Mountains

A brick factory

Laotian foreign technical experts and government officials.

Most Laotian industries are in or near Vientiane. There is a concrete plant at Van Vieng and nearby the Nam Ngum Dam. Other small factories cut plywood and make detergents. Some places are just a step beyond a family shop with only two or three employees.

The best schools, both high schools and the university, are also in Vientiane. Families that are able, often send their teenage sons or daughters to live in the city and go to school.

The most famous wat in Vientiane is Wat Sisaket, which keeps the three Pitaka, the most sacred books of the Buddhist religion. In hollows of the walls sit thousands of miniature Buddhas. Hundreds of larger Buddhas made of bronze line the floor. Colorful angels and flowers are carved into the pillars, the walls, and the ceiling.

23

The larger cities in Laos all have a great variety of markets and shops.

THAKHEK

South of Vientiane, the mountains of the Annamite chain become limestone. Sinkholes and streams appear and then disappear into nowhere. Cities cluster like beads on a string along the Mekong. Thakhek is a lumber and mining town lying across the river from Thailand only 80 miles (129 kilometers) from Vietnam. Its location and river port make the city a focus of activity. Even its name is an invitation for trade: *tha* means port and *khek* means guest.

SAVANNAKHET

Another fifty miles (eighty kilometers) down the Mekong sits Savannakhet, the marketplace of south Laos and the second-largest city in the country. Mangos, coconut palms, and champac trees guard rows of small Chinese-owned shops. The household works below and lives up above. Before the war, hardware stores sold nets for fishing, nails, and axes, things not easily made in the villages. Pharmacies carried both Western medicines and small boxes of sharp-smelling herbs for soothing, curing teas. For a quick stop before work or at lunch, there were shops offering iced coffee and others featuring the Indochinese specialty: bowls of soup-noodles. However, the war has caused many of the Chinese shop owners to leave. Some of the stores are still shuttered and closed while others have new businesses under old signs. Cooking charcoal is for sale on the corners, taking advantage of the shortage of kerosene. State-owned stores sell a little of everything, trying to supply the basics to the city. The streets have few private cars since gasoline and parts are not easily available.

Occasional open-sided buses still clatter out toward villages nearby. Some green Soviet-made cars pass importantly, scattering bicycles and pedestrians. The *samloas*, or "three wheels," act as taxis. These modified motorcycles, with an added seat and wheel, are able to find gasoline when no one else can. Savannakhet's most impressive transportation is by air. It was an aviation training center during the war. Its airfields are among the few that can land jets. Anyone wishing to come in or out of the panhandle of Laos passes through Savannakhet.

THE MEKONG PASSES THROUGH THE JUNGLE

Below Savannakhet, the Mekong turns from a quiet carrier of boats into a series of waterfalls and rapids. The forest becomes jungle. Weather alternates between dry heat and wet heat. Even in

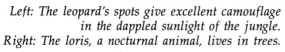

Left: The leopard's spots give excellent camouflage in the dappled sunlight of the jungle.
Right: The loris, a nocturnal animal, lives in trees.

December, it can climb to 70 degrees Fahrenheit (23.9 degrees Celsius), and in the summer, it is often over 100 degrees Fahrenheit (37.8 degrees Celsius). In certain areas there are more than 160 inches (406 centimeters) of rain each year. July and August are the wettest months, although only eight to ten weeks a year can really be called dry. The trees are thick and tall, the first layer forming a continuous canopy 110 feet (34 meters) above the forest floor. At 60 feet (18 meters) lies a lower blanket of leaves. Orchids and ferns wrap tree trunks and liana vines snake their way far up the branches. There are animals too, niding between the shadows and the sunlight: leopards, tigers, king cobras, crocodiles, rhinoceroses, scaly anteaters, and monkeylike loris with their huge eyes and woolly fur.

THE BOLOVENS PLATEAU

Out beyond the jungle are the fertile grasslands and the more mild temperatures of the Bolovens Plateau. Coffee beans are cultivated here along with tea, rubber trees, and fields of tobacco. The plateau is famous for its pineapples and rich, red strawberries.

During the rainy season, many roads are almost impassable.

The beautiful, rolling hills have attracted settlement since ancient times. The fabled Kingdom of Champa began here in the second century. By a quiet lake near the jungle, a visitor can still climb the mossy stone steps of the thousand-year-old Wat Phu.

PAKSE

Just north of Wat Phu is the city of Pakse. About the same size as Savannakhet, it is the last major city before the border with Cambodia. Pakse is a farming town, a combination of modern construction and growth, and narrow, red dirt streets. The Mekong and Se Done rivers flow through the center of the city, separating it into two parts connected by a graceful bridge. South of the city, islands dot the Mekong and rocky waterfalls stream down from the heights of cliffs.

While the countryside of Laos is diverse and beautiful, its history has been marked by war and conflict.

27

Chapter 3

LAN XANG—THE LAND OF A MILLION ELEPHANTS

THE LEGEND OF KHUN BOROM

Riding on a pure white elephant with transparent tusks and ebony eyes, the noble Khun Borom is said to have descended from the heavens. His two wives preceded him. Behind followed a procession of water buffalo, horses, elephants, wise men, soldiers, servants, and music makers. Khun Borom was the first Lao monarch.

This legend, polished with centuries of retelling, describes the entry of the Tai people into the kingdom of Laos. A mixture of truth and myth, it recounts the journey of Khun Borom from the eighth century Tai homelands of southern China into the northern Laotian mountains. According to Chinese history, his followers were not Chinese but *Nan Tiao*, ''People of the South.'' They lived in small settlements that were ruled by lords, called *tiao*. Villagers supported the tiao who, in turn, paid tribute to Chinese officials. There are records from China dating back to the second and third centuries that record victories and defeats of the Nan Tiao armies.

Opposite page: An Asiatic elephant

The legend continues. Khun Borom found a huge pumpkin magically appearing on a great liana vine. Curious, he pierced the pumpkin with a red-hot poker. Through the hole fell seeds blackened with ash. These became the Lao Theung, the first people to live in Laos. Then, scattering upon the earth were the lighter seeds of the Lao Lum tribes and the Lao aristocracy.

Khun Borom took his armies and settled at the northern edges of the land. There he produced seven sons, and in the tradition of the times, sent each out to establish a kingdom. Khun Lo, the oldest, built his city near the site of present-day Luang Prabang.

THE KHMER PEOPLE, THE LAO THEUNG

These first Tai did not come into an empty country. The darker seeds of the pumpkin refer to the Khmer people, Lao Theung, who had settled by the Mekong River. It is thought they may have crossed the seas from Indonesia, some remaining in Cambodia and others continuing up the Mekong to the rich lowlands of Laos. The Lao Theung were no match for the stronger new invaders. The Tai named them *Kha* (slave), and forced them up into the hills. As Tai ancestors had bowed to the Chinese in Nan Tiao, now the Lao Theung were forced to bow to the Tai, paying tribute and donating labor at harvest.

KING FA NGUM

The twenty-second king in 1353 was Fa Ngum. Fa Ngum is probably the most famous person in Lao history. Storytellers have recounted his life so many times that fantasy has woven itself inseparably into fact. Every Lao child has heard how he was born with thirty-two teeth. The court was terrified of this omen of

Art depicting the royal elephant of Lan Xang

misfortune. The king, Fa Ngum's grandfather, exiled father and son, leaving them on a raft to float down the Mekong into Cambodia. When the raft washed up onto a riverbank, they were rescued by a friendly Buddhist monk. He sheltered them for seven years. The king of Cambodia learned of the two princes and brought them into his court. Fa Ngum eventually married the king's daughter.

At twenty-four, the young Fa Ngum set out to regain his throne. His army marched up the river valleys and through the mountains reaching the Laotian kingdom. Fa Ngum then issued a challenge to battle. After a brutal clash of men and elephants, Fa Ngum had defeated his grandfather's armies. In 1353, he proclaimed himself king. The court's predictions of misfortune had come true.

During the next twenty years, Fa Ngum marched and captured territory throughout the Indochinese Peninsula. His empire was called *Lan Xang*, or the "Land of a Million Elephants."

Early engraving of a temple in Luang Prabang

It is said Fa Ngum was responsible for the growth of Therevada Buddhism in Laos. He requested from his father-in-law, the king of Cambodia, priests, books, and the priceless Golden Buddha, the Prabang. He built temples and men traveled from the outskirts of the kingdom to study Buddhism.

Fa Ngum became more and more powerful. He had armies of forty-eight thousand men and five hundred elephants. His name caused fear and respect. But along with power came pride. Fa Ngum grew careless and cruel. His generals first began to speak and then to plot against him. In 1373, Fa Ngum was again exiled and died.

FA NGUM'S SUCCESSORS EXPAND THEIR TERRITORY

Oun Hueun, Fa Ngum's son, succeeded him as ruler. Oun Hueun called himself *Samsenethai,* or "Ruler of the Three Hundred Thousand Tai." Samsenethai ruled more than forty years. Under him and the kings of the next two centuries, Laos continued to expand. Yunnan Province, the original home of the Tai, parts of southern China, the Shan States of Burma, northern Cambodia, northern Thailand, and the edges of Vietnam all became part of the Laotian Kingdom, Lan Xang.

By the middle of the fifteenth century, Lan Xang was the most powerful nation in the Indochinese Peninsula. The succeeding centuries brought both victory and defeat. Lan Xang's borders swelled and fell back again.

The first Europeans came to Laos in 1641. These missionaries and merchants found a peaceful country ruled by King Souligna Vongsa. His fifty-seven years of rule, known as the Golden Age of Laos, were marked by compromise instead of force. At one time a disagreement arose over a boundary between Laos and Vietnam. Souligna proposed that since the Laotians built their houses on stilts and the Vietnamese on the ground, the division of the countries would be drawn between the two kinds of dwellings. It was agreed upon and war was avoided.

TROUBLE IN THE KINGDOM OF LAN XANG

Souligna Vongsa left no son. When he died, a battle for control began. In 1707, after four hundred years of existence, the kingdom of Lan Xang broke in two. Vientiane was captured by one ruler, another controlled Luang Prabang. By 1717, Champassak had broken away to form a third nation. The tiny, mountainous area of Xieng Khouang paid tribute both to Vietnam and the three other more powerful Laotian kingdoms. One surviving record listing three years of gifts to Vietnam includes four hundred bars of silver, ten elephants, and thirteen rhino horns.

LAOS IS DEFEATED

As Laos became weaker its kingdoms quarreled among themselves, and the surrounding states saw opportunities for invasion. At various times Thailand, Vietnam, Burma, and Cambodia promised help and threatened attack. In 1778, Thailand conquered Champassak and Vientiane. Hundreds of families were forced to resettle south in Sayaboury under Thailand's control. The royal court from Vientiane was removed to Bangkok, Thailand's capital. For the next thirty years, Laos was Thailand's unwilling ally in war and partner in trade. In 1824 the Laotian ruler of Vientiane, Tiao Anou, persuaded the Thai to put his son on the throne of Champassak. With the strength of two kingdoms and help from Vietnam, Tiao Anou betrayed his Thai supporters and invaded. He was beaten. When he attacked again in 1828, Thailand marched to Vientiane in anger and razed it. Forty years later, a group of explorers from France reached Vientiane to find only crumbling ruins and forest.

Xieng Khouang during this time had been balancing favors and threats from the surrounding powers. It aligned itself with Vietnam, but sent gifts and promises to Thailand. When Tiao Anou fled to Xieng Khouang, there was no choice but to offend either Thailand or Vietnam. Tiao Anou was surrendered to Thailand. Vietnam struck in reprisal, taking over the tiny country.

The French capture a Laotian city.

The occupation was cruel, but short-lived. In 1865, another power stronger than any on the Indochinese Peninsula appeared on the scene.

THE FRENCH ARRIVE IN INDOCHINA

France was looking for new territories. The British had colonies and control in Burma and India. They used these countries as a gateway to China and Chinese trade. France found itself paying England for goods that came from the Far East. In addition there was a centuries-old rivalry between the two countries. It seemed only appropriate that France should have colonies too. Vietnam was weak and available. At first the French sent only priests and traders. When disagreements occurred, France sent an army. In 1883 the Vietnamese Royal House agreed to all French demands, and the French Protectorate in Vietnam was established.

A group of rebels who helped force the French out of Indochina

THE FRENCH CONQUER VIETNAM

Conquering territory, however, was far different from keeping it. In contrast to the first adventuring chieftains who governed only as much as they could control sending out their sons to invade new lands, modern colonial powers ruled from afar. A few people remained to administer taxes and conduct trade, but their authority was largely confined to the cities. The mountains were sources of unrest and new rebellion. This was the situation facing the French in Vietnam.

Within a few years the mountains of Laos on the Vietnamese border held three groups allied against the French. Defiant officials from the Vietnamese royal court joined tribal armies regrouping from a rebellion in China. A mixture of clans calling themselves the Tai Tribal Federation combined to attack French

36

outposts. The French responded with force. A cycle of revolt began, crushed by the French military only to arise again in another place. This continued until the French were finally forced out of Indochina fifty years later.

AUGUSTE PAVIE

On September 30, 1886, a Frenchman named Auguste Pavie crossed into Laos with eight aides from Cambodia. He came to explore, not to fight. Monsieur Pavie had arrived in Indochina in 1869 as a sergeant in the French army. He was fascinated by the country. Pavie had traveled as a survey geographer where no European had ever been, recording his thoughts and discoveries in a journal. The French had colonized Vietnam, but most of Laos was still separate, dependent on Thailand. On this September day, Pavie was trying to arrange a meeting with the seventy-six-year-old king of Luang Prabang, Oun Kham. It was difficult because Thailand, also battling the Hos and the Tai Federation, distrusted anyone from France.

It was not until Thailand withdrew from Luang Prabang several months later that Pavie had his chance. The Thai forces took hostages with them from the ruling Deos of the Tai Federation. Deo Van Tri waited, then swept into Luang Prabang taking revenge for his brothers' kidnapping. Deo drove off the remaining Thai troops and destroyed the city. The old king was trapped in the flaming palace. Auguste Pavie and his aides rescued the king from the flames and commandeered a boat to carry him safely down the Mekong.

Several months later the king signed a document transferring the loyalties of Luang Prabang from Thailand to France. The first step in the French occupation of Laos had been taken. Now the French Syndicate of Laos, inspired by Pavie's writings, was formed in France by wealthy scholars and businessmen. They supplied Pavie with money and men to begin scientific exploration of Laos and to continue contacts with local officials. The reports convinced France more and more of Laos's potential value.

THE FRENCH TAKE OVER LAOS

Thailand had been weakened by its constant wars. When a dispute in 1893 sent French gunboats to the port of Bangkok, the Thais agreed to relinquish control over Laos, east of the Mekong River, to France. By 1907 all Laos was officially a French protectorate living under a French administration and following French law.

The French took over a Laos that had not known unity since 1700. Lan Xang, "The Land of a Million Elephants," had died with its ruler Souligna Vongsa. Each of the pieces of the realm, Vientiane, Luang Prabang, Champassak, and tiny Xieng Khouang had its own king, its own group of languages, and its own customs.

The French rejoined these parts and called the whole *Laos*, from the name of one of the major tribes, the Lawas. New boundaries were drawn. The Mekong River now defined the country on one side and the Annamite Mountain chain on the other. The remaining regions were joined to Thailand or Vietnam. Thus, of the approximately twenty million Laotians in Southeast Asia, only three-and-a-half million of them lived in Laos. Often citizens on one side of the border are ethnically identical to those living on the other side.

The palace in Luang Prabang, built by the French in the nineteenth century

THE FRENCH SET UP A GOVERNMENT

Auguste Pavie was the first French governor of the new Laos. It was a natural choice since his adventures and enthusiastic support had involved the French in Laos originally. Pavie brought with him about seventy Frenchmen to take over the highest positions in the government. Vietnamese officials occupied the next rung. Below them the provinces and the villages were led by traditional chiefs elected under Laotian versions of French democracy.

The king of Luang Prabang was named king of the country. All the traditions and splendor of the palace were encouraged, but the king's actual power was quite limited. Major decisions were made by the French. The remaining royalty of the other kingdoms of Laos had to accept lesser positions. Often the French administration would choose members of one tribe to act as tax collectors or district officers for another tribe. A Lamet village might have to deal with a Lu agent who, in turn, was under a Lao administrator. The administrator would be responsible to a Vietnamese superior under orders himself from a French official. Resentment over taxes and controls was deflected from the French and directed toward the foreign tribal authority.

The French found that colonial rule, especially in Laos, was more trouble than profit. Their dreams of a gateway to China, trade with a Lao population of more than two million, and exports of iron and precious metals never became reality. The Mekong River with its rocks and rapids was useless on long journeys of exploration and trade. The villagers were more accustomed to dealing with Chinese peddlers than French businessmen. Many Lao villages made or grew almost everything they needed and were not particularly interested in trade at all. The mountains made travel by land and development of mines or agriculture very difficult. Laos never supplied more than 1 percent of the total French exports from Indochina.

France felt, however, that it could not leave Laos. French national honor and competition between European powers were factors, but most important, Laos provided protection. It was a buffer, a mountainous space separating areas under French rule from areas under English rule. Control of Laos also meant control of the mountains on the borders of French Vietnam. It was vital to keep these rocky hiding places out of the hands of rebels from the much more profitable Vietnamese colony.

So the French and their Vietnamese administrators stayed in Laos. Laotian children went to school to learn their lessons in French. The French national anthem was sung and the French flag flew with the Laotian flag over the royal palace.

TAXES, BUT FEW IMPROVEMENTS

To support the administration in Laos, the Assembly in France voted new taxes on Lao citizens. Not only money, but donations of agricultural products and a certain amount of free labor was required each year. When the demands were more than a village could afford, there was revolt. Often, to avoid trouble, the French administrators made no real effort to collect, especially in more remote areas.

In contrast to the energies that the French invested in Vietnam, Laos was generally ignored. A few roads were constructed. The tin mine in Khammouan Province near Thakhek was developed. The cities, especially Vientiane, built governmental buildings of French colonial architecture with French funds. Mostly, however, Laos remained predictable, quiet, and undeveloped.

JAPAN BECOMES AGGRESSIVE

In 1931, Manchuria, a region of China near the Soviet Union, was occupied by Japan. No one in the surrounding countries knew where Japan's force would be felt next. Unease and uncertainty filled Asia. It was at this time that Charles Rochet came to Laos. He was a Frenchman, like Auguste Pavie, intensely interested in Lao history and culture.

Pointing to Japan's aggression, Charles Rochet told French authorities that Laos needed a stronger national identity to increase its will to defend itself. The French, although they had unified Laos, had always treated it as a blend of tribes and kingdoms. Even the Laotian flag showed three elephants on a pedestal representing the three states of Vientiane, Luang

Prabang, and Champassak. Now Charles Rochet convinced the French administration to change their approach. The Lao Association was started where children could learn Lao music and dance. Schools were built. A newspaper written in the Lao language was begun. There were patriotic programs and parades. The children learned the history of the Lan Xang kingdom. Some of them and their parents began to imagine that Lan Xang could return.

WORLD WAR II

Meanwhile, the world had become a very hostile place. Japan's influence in Asia grew. The territories conquered by Japan's armies expanded in an ever-widening circle. There was war in Europe, too. Adolf Hitler, the leader in Germany, attacked Czechoslovakia in 1938 and marched into Poland in 1939. By 1940 Germany had invaded and occupied France. Most of the French in Laos were sent home, replaced by new Frenchmen that Germany thought it could trust. Admiral Jean Decoux took over as governor-general of Laos. Like so many leaders of Laos before, he tried to balance and satisfy the powers within and without Laos. Thailand attacked the weakened French-Laotian government in 1940. This short Franco-Thai War was ended by the landing of Japanese troops. Admiral Decoux felt he had no choice but to cooperate with Japan's forces.

Opium had always been exported from Laos, both as an addicting drug and as a medicine. It had been quietly profitable to the French and the hill tribes that grew it. Now that the war had interfered with much of the other opium production in Indochina, the plant had become extremely valuable. The French combed the

Admiral Jean Decoux

hills and bargained with opium-producing tribes. Feuds over opium trade began the present-day split of the clans into opposing groups.

END OF WORLD WAR II

Some Frenchmen disagreed with Admiral Decoux's policy of compromise with the Japanese. French paratroopers secretly dropped into the hills. They made guerrilla raids on Japanese command posts. Japan reacted. In March 1945, Japan abruptly declared Laos independent of French rule and arrested French officials. Vietnamese were given the positions that the French had held. Five months later, in August, the United States dropped an atomic bomb on Japan. The war in Asia was over. Japan signed a total surrender. Laos was neither free nor occupied. A power struggle began between the new nationalistic leaders in Laos and France trying to reclaim the country. Thailand and Vietnam stood back and waited to choose sides.

In Vientiane a farmer uses his yoked cattle for transportation (below), while youngsters use bicycles (above). Both are common forms of transport in Laos.

Chapter 4

THE CONFLICTS
OF INDEPENDENCE

The war was over. For the first time in over two hundred years, there was no foreign force in Laos. The Japanese had thrown out the French and now Japan had been expelled. Thailand, Vietnam, and China, long occupiers of Laos, remained within their borders recovering from their own war wounds. Laos was free and determined to retain that freedom.

ORGANIZING AN INDEPENDENT NATION

While France was in Laos, all the higher governmental posts were given to French or Vietnamese. Positions on the next level were occupied by Laotian royalty and a few wealthy families. These were the Laotian elite. They sent their children to be educated in France and had ideas that were as much Western as Laotian. They had little in common with the people of Laos.

Most of the elite felt Laos could not survive without military and financial aid from a stronger power. Those who looked to France and the West for this support were called rightists. Those who trusted the Soviet Union and China were called leftists. Some people felt that Laos should be open to help from all sides without committing itself to any. These were the neutralists. Many of the elite in Laos were afraid of Vietnam and its past history of aggression. Others were more afraid of France and resentful of colonial rule.

The population of Laos was just as divided. Chinese and Vietnamese filled the cities, some had lived in Laos for generations. They had their own schools, spoke their own language, and identified with the nations of their ancestors. Sixty different clans made up the rest of the country. Each wanted its own secure place in the new order.

ROYAL HOUSE OF LUANG PRABANG TAKES OVER

Two brothers, Prince Phetsarath and Souvanna Phouma, along with their half-brother, Souphanouvong, held the power in Laos from 1945 to 1975. They belonged to the royal house of Luang Prabang, part of a family of several wives and twenty sons. The brothers became the most influential leaders in Laos, whether working together or in conflict, for three decades.

Because of his determination and great physical strength, Prince Phetsarath was known as the Iron Man. The first of the brothers, born in 1890, he chose to study in England. When the Japanese left Laos in 1945, Prince Phetsarath seized the opportunity to try to unify the country under Laotian rule.

Souvanna Phouma believed in compromise. His enemies accused him of "bending whichever way the wind blew." They claimed Souvanna Phouma's support was always available to the strongest side. Most Laotians felt Phouma held the nation together when no one else could. He called himself a neutralist, his only

Left to right, signing an agreement: Princes Boun Oum, Souvanna Phouma, and Souphanouvong

cause that of his country. Born in 1901 and trained as an electrical engineer and architect in France, Phouma was as comfortable negotiating with guerrilla fighters as he was with diplomats. He served as premier of Laos five times. Many Laotians listened to Souvanna Phouma and believed in his goal of finding the possible in the conflicts of his times.

Souphanouvong, the youngest of the three, was born in 1909. They all shared the same father, but Souphanouvong's mother was not from a royal family. People claimed this, and his jealousy toward his older brothers, was why he sympathized with the common people instead of the nobility. Souphanouvong studied in France and, while there, became attracted to Communism as a possible solution to Laos's problems. When Souphanouvong returned, he was sent by the French Road Commission to design

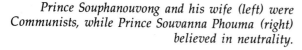

Prince Souphanouvong and his wife (left) were Communists, while Prince Souvanna Phouma (right) believed in neutrality.

bridges in Vietnam. There, he married a Vietnamese girl and became seriously involved in nationalist and Communist groups. By 1947 he had become the spokesman for their cause, and nicknamed the "Red Prince."

THE FRENCH RETURN

Independence for Laos under Japan changed the political situation very little. French officials were replaced by a few Japanese and the administrative role of the Vietnamese was strengthened. For convenience, the capital was moved to Thakhek. When Japan hastily pulled out of Indochina in 1945, France sent a polite note to Prince Phetsarath stating that the French would be returning and life would resume much as it had been before the war. The prince replied that Laos was now a free country and the French were no longer welcome. The old king, anxious to avoid trouble, countermanded Prince Phetsarath's order. Phetsarath deposed the king. With speed and efficiency, the French dispatched their troops up the Mekong and dropped paratroopers at various locations throughout the country. A year later, in April 1946, there was a last quick, bloody battle at Thakhek and the French resumed control. Prince Phetsarath, Souvanna Phouma, Souphanouvong, and most of the educated elite fled to Thailand to start a government in exile.

By 1949, the French had agreed to give Laos internal autonomy. The exiles were invited to return. Most accepted. Souphanouvong angrily rejected the offer and journeyed to Vietnam to join anti-French Laotian rebels. Prince Phetsarath, equally distrusting French and Vietnamese, remained in Thailand.

FRENCH WAR IN INDOCHINA

North Vietnam mounted a resistance against the French return, resulting in what was called the French War in Indochina. Souphanouvong was determined to bring this resistance into Laos and formed the Pathet Lao dedicated to Laotian independence. Souvanna Phouma, now premier of Laos, was caught between the radical nationalists and the French. Pathet Lao guerrillas began their attacks against units of the Royal Laotian army.

CEASE-FIRE CONFERENCE

By 1954, after eight years of Indochinese conflict, no side had won. The United States now provided the primary financial support for the pro-Western Laotian government's fight against the guerrillas. With American backing, a conference was called in Geneva, Switzerland, to arrange a cease-fire. Britain, the U.S.S.R., the U.S.A., France, Laos, China, Cambodia, and Vietnam participated. Neither the Pathet Lao nor a similar rebel group in Cambodia was allowed to send delegates. They were considered arms of the Vietnamese Communists, not representative groups of their countries. At the conclusion of the conference, Vietnam was partitioned into a Communist north and a pro-Western south. Laos was designated as a neutral state. Two northern Laotian provinces, Sam Neua and Phong Saly, were put under Pathet Lao control. Pathet Lao troops were instructed to disband or join the regular Laotian army. A United Nations commission made up of India, Poland, and Canada arrived to supervise the cease-fire.

LAOS TRIES TO FORM A COALITION GOVERNMENT

By 1956 guerrilla attacks and government response had brought Laos back to the edge of civil war. Souvanna Phouma proposed peace in the form of a coalition government with members from both sides. The coalition retained Phouma as premier and included two Pathet Lao cabinet ministers. Souphanouvong was put in charge of economic planning. The first elections to include the Pathet Lao were held in February 1958. Surprisingly the Pathet Lao won thirteen out of the twenty-one new seats up for election in the National Assembly. This was only thirteen out of a total of fifty-nine elected places, but the Pathet Lao's strength shocked the rightists and the Western powers. The United States showed its concern and displeasure by withdrawing financial aid.

RIGHTISTS GAIN CONTROL

The next crisis occurred at the ceremony to combine the two Pathet Lao battalions into the Royal Government troops. It was rumored that the rebels were to be scattered throughout the army with written tests determining their rank. The uneducated Pathet Lao felt betrayed. When the time arrived for the ceremony, the Pathet Lao soldiers came with their weapons loaded. They were immediately surrounded by the Royal Government forces. By the next morning one of the battalions had flowed through the government lines and disappeared. The pro-Western administration in Vientiane was furious. Violence flared. In July the last Pathet Lao battalion escaped into the jungle. Souphanouvong and over one hundred of his supporters were arrested. The rightists forces, with support from the United States Central Intelligence Agency (CIA), removed Souvanna Phouma and took control of the government. The elections in 1960 were arranged so that the right won all fifty-nine seats.

THE GOVERNMENT IS OVERTHROWN

Disgusted with the situation, Kong Le, a five-foot-two-inch captain from the Lao Theung hill tribes, decided to take action. Kong Le had been strongly influenced by both sides. His favorite teacher in high school had become a Pathet Lao Communist leader. But his military education had been with the French and Americans in the Philippine Islands. He was now a commander of an elite parachute battalion. Kong Le's wife was the niece of the rightist general who had become premier. With a call of "Laotians must stop fighting Laotians," Kong Le mobilized the army and overthrew the government. He offered the premiership to Souvanna Phouma, who accepted.

In the meantime, Souphanouvong had convinced his guards to help him escape. He and all his followers took refuge in Vietnam.

The Geneva Conference of 1962

The country was now divided into three groups: the rightists, the neutralists under Souvanna Phouma, and the leftists under Souphanouvong. Each side had its soldiers and its supporters. Laos was torn with bloodshed. In 1962, negotiations among the United States, France, Britain, and the Soviet Union led to the second Geneva Conference.

THE GENEVA CONFERENCE OF 1962

At the Geneva Conference in 1962, unlike the first conference in 1954, there was a great effort to encourage the participation of all the countries and parties involved. Both conferences, however, concluded with very similar results. Laos was to be neutral. No foreign troops were to be stationed in the country and those there were ordered to leave. Another Control Commission was organized and a new coalition government representing all three sides was created. Souvanna Phouma and Souphanouvong were included along with a rightist representative, the royal head of Champassak, Prince Boun Oum. This new effort lasted a year. Early in 1963, after the assassination of several top leftist officials, the coalition was broken by fear and distrust. Souphanouvong once again fled to Vietnam.

LAOS BECOMES INVOLVED IN THE VIETNAM WAR

Although the United States had been active in Laos for more than ten years, events were quickly coming together to trigger a dramatic increase in United States involvement. The war between South Vietnam and the North Vietnamese Communists had intensified. The United States had stepped in where France had stepped out in 1954. In 1961 American troops began combat in Vietnam. The Ho Chi Minh Trail in the Laotian mountains fed supplies to the South Vietnamese Communists. A special United States Air Warfare Unit in Thailand trained Lao and Thai pilots to conduct strikes against the trails and the Pathet Lao. In December 1964, there were more than three thousand United States Air Force personnel and seventy-five aircraft stationed in Laos. In 1965, over forty-five hundred air strikes had been made in northern Laos and more in southern Laos. By 1971 the jets were bombing at a rate of seven hundred to one thousand missions a day. There were no more attempts to compromise. Laos was committed to war until one side or the other was victorious.

Prince Phetsarath had died in 1960, still stubbornly anti-French, anti-American, and anti-Communist. Kong Le was removed from

Captain Kong Le, photographed here in his paratrooper uniform, was removed from command in 1966.

command in 1966 and, feeling betrayed, left for Indonesia. He was to return, this time on the side of the Pathet Lao. A few of the more extreme rightists made some last attempts at a coup and then escaped to Thailand. Souvanna Phouma remained to reluctantly support the United States.

The elite and most of the lowland Lao Lum supported the West. The Lao Theung hill people were the backbone of the Pathet Lao troops. They felt no loyalty to the Royal Laotian government, which had neglected them. The Hmong on the ridges of the mountains were divided much along the same lines as in the opium feud before the war. When American fliers were shot down on their secret bombing missions across the Ho Chi Minh Trail, the pro-Western Hmong rescued them and brought them to safety. As time passed, the United States trained and paid these Hmong who developed into skillful, tough fighters. They were strong, independent, and knew the mountains.

*The United States poured money into Laos, but
it was not used to help or equip the fighting forces.*

and the Western powers. Through persuasion and force, the
Pathet Lao was winning the countryside. Desperate, the United
States poured more and more money into the country. Forty
million dollars a year flowed into Laos providing total support for
the military and propping up the national economy. Much of the
aid never went where it was intended to go. Generals drove
expensive cars and built elaborate villas. Bribes became a natural
way of doing business. Eight hundred thousand people were
homeless, one-fourth of the population. The Pathet Lao promised
peace, freedom, and equality. Four-fifths of the land and two-
fifths of the population were controlled by the Pathet Lao in 1972.

THE PATHET LAO GAINS POWER IN LAOS

At the end of 1973, Souvanna Phouma appealed to the Pathet
Lao to try a coalition government once again. They agreed. This

The Pathet Lao forces were a powerful, disciplined group.

time the government was organized with exactly half the power and positions going to each side, from the smallest village to the National Assembly. There was debate and stormy disagreement, but it seemed the government might survive. Then in 1975 Vietnam fell to the Communists. Abruptly the Americans pulled out of both Vietnam and Laos. The American air force made massive efforts to airlift Hmong soldiers and their families out of the country.

Students at the universities held demonstrations calling for the Pathet Lao to take complete control. Government workers panicked and fled. The Pathet Lao, including Prince Souphanouvong, assumed power. Souvanna Phouma, now seventy-four years old, was made an adviser to the new Communist government. The six-hundred-year-old monarchy ended.

Chapter 5

A COMMUNIST COUNTRY

"Laos is free. The American imperialists no longer control us. We must cooperate, sacrifice together to build a country of strength and equality."

The loudspeakers on the corners of the streets blared promises and blamed the past for all the problems of Laos. People listened; some in hope or belief, some in panic. Most, weary of war, listened without emotion or commitment. This was the new government. They must learn to live with it.

At first it seemed the monarchy would be saved, but the antigovernment forces had used the king as a rallying cry. It was not long before King Savang Vatthana and the seven hundred years of royalty that he represented were gone. Policy was made by a central committee chaired by Kaysone Phomvihane. Born to a Vietnamese father and a Laotian mother, he was a symbol of the new special relationship between Laos and Vietnam. Fifteen of the forty-five committee members had been with the Communist party since its formation in Laos thirty years earlier. Four were women, including Chairman Kaysone's wife. One was a Hmong, Faydang Lobliayao. One, Sisomphone Louansay, was a tribal Tai.

Although almost two-thirds of the guerrilla army had been Lao Theung, there were no Lao Theung on the highest levels of the ruling body. Whatever the government decided was law.

Troops from the former Pathet Lao provinces and the Lao Theung strongholds along with Vietnamese soldiers patrolled the streets. Their instructions were to be helpful and friendly—to convince the citizens of the government's good intentions. But the Lao Theung were farmers and men of the hills not familiar with city ways. Their Lao was awkward and their knowledge limited. The people made fun of the soldiers behind their backs and resented their orders.

Laos had always been divided into governmental units: the provinces, the cities, and the towns down to groups of ten families with a unit leader. This leader traditionally registered births and took care of small record-keeping functions. Now he was given great new powers. His permission was needed to travel, to purchase livestock, or to receive rations of rice. He asked and reported to his superiors: "Where were you last night? Who visited your house? Why were you late to work?" In the evening, the street was closed with a bamboo gate and a sentry. If there was an emergency, a stick was lighted to signal for help. Frequently, mass meetings, or *semmana*, were held presenting the new policies of the regime. The unit leader was responsible for the attendance of his neighborhood.

REJECTION OF WESTERN INFLUENCE

Speakers at the semmana condemned the corruption and weakness of the old Royal Laotian government and its Western advisers. Foreign culture was ridiculed. Rock music, blue jeans,

Communist soldiers on patrol

high heels, long hair for men, or short permed hair for women—
all were forbidden. Past officials were criticized and the audience
was encouraged to join in the accusations. If the official was there,
he rose and criticized himself. "Capitalism is a disease," said the
speaker. "These are good people, but they are sick. We must cure
them through education." Former police, high-ranking soldiers,
and government personnel met with smiling authorities
sympathetic to the problems of adjustment. "Just a few months at
a reeducation camp on the northern borders of Laos and Vietnam
and you may go home," they were promised. Some people
volunteered to go to the camps hoping after a few months of
training they could return to a position in the new government.
Sometimes there was no choice. Soldiers came at night, and in the
morning the person would be gone.

REEDUCATION CAMPS

The reeducation camps were set in valleys. On the hills above, North Vietnamese or Lao Theung troops kept guard. The soldiers were young, fourteen and fifteen years old, and taught to kill anyone trying to escape. Former police officials and the elite of the old government now spent the day cutting down the jungle, building huts, and hoeing plots of vegetables. Cameras, compasses, maps, and radios were not allowed. Work and rice were shared within a group. If one member did not contribute, the rest suffered. Every night lecturers criticized the old regime, accusing it of enriching itself at the expense of the country. Time passed. Most people stayed in the camps at least four or five years. Some are still there.

Back in the cities and the countryside, the Communists felt constantly threatened. The population was distrustful. Resistance groups roamed the hills and formed guerrilla camps on the borders. It was not safe to travel country roads at night. The Communist government flew bombing raids killing thousands, especially among the rebelling Hmong. By 1979, fifteen thousand people had spent time in reeducation camps, but the country was still not secure.

REFUGEES POUR OUT OF LAOS

The economy was weak; the weather was bad; people were hungry. Refugees—almost 124,000 in 1970—poured across the Mekong into Thailand. Some bought space on boats running an illegal, dangerous taxi service across the river. Others swam. Whole families floated across in huge tires taken from military

Evacuating refugees by helicopter

trucks or tied themselves to tree trunks to be carried along the current. Sometimes soldiers along the riverbanks shot and killed the escapees. Sometimes the soldiers were bribed. Sometimes they tried not to see.

Thailand set up refugee camps not only for the Laotians, but also fleeing Vietnamese and Cambodians. The camps were like crowded cities full of displaced people who had nothing to do but wait. Thailand was overwhelmed. The Thais felt that the Western powers who had helped cause the problems now were unwilling to do their share in supporting the camps and resettling the refugees. There were times when Thailand closed its borders and arrested refugees and put them in jail. Thai military craft would patrol the Mekong turning the escaping boats back toward Laos. When promises of help and resettlement came from the United States and other Western countries, Thailand's borders reopened and the struggle to feed, shelter, and find homes for the refugees continued.

During the war, allies of both the Soviet Union and China had supplied Vietnam and the Pathet Lao with money and arms. In 1977 Vietnam invaded and occupied Cambodia driving out the cruel Chinese-supported government there. The Chinese felt not only betrayed, but also threatened by the growing Vietnamese power. China turned from an ally to an enemy. Chinese help to Vietnam stopped. Chinese provinces became a shelter for defecting officials and generals, a center for training resistance groups.

THE GOVERNMENT TRIES TO HELP IMPROVE AND REBUILD LAOS

The Laotian government strained to keep its promises while repressing its enemies. Teachers and health teams were briefly trained and given what supplies were available. Soldiers, farmers, and advisers joined to build schools, health dispensaries, and irrigation projects in the villages. State stores and state farms gradually took the place of private ownership. Disagreement with government policy was labeled misunderstanding.

Worship of the *phi*, spirits that the Laotians believe hide in every mountain crevice, forest, or hut, was condemned as backward superstition.

The philosophy of Buddhism was encouraged. The Communists pointed out similarities between the Buddhist religion and the Communist philosophy. Both preached equality among people, revolt against unfair masters, and an end to suffering. Buddhism valued harmony, understanding, and acceptance. The

Communists stressed the importance of class conflict and material possessions. These were not seen as opposing views, but were considered different approaches to the same goals. The government tried to influence the monks to emphasize the practical side of their religion. They were encouraged to teach, plant gardens, and help the sick instead of studying religious texts or meditating.

But by 1979 Laos was near collapse. For every change, there was resistance. For every act of kindness or step of progress made by the government, there was also an act of harshness or repression. The refugee flow could not be stopped. Even in government ministries, there was opposition and corruption. Government salaries were so low that officials looked for bribes and sold influence. Political disputes divided the ruling councils. Some members wanted to mend ties with China, while the majority favored continuing the alliance with Russia. Arguments were made for relaxing government restrictions. Other arguments demanded strong measures to bring the country under control. Disagreement brought arrest, public charges, and more flight from the country.

At the end of 1979, under the guidance of the Soviet Union, Chairman Kaysone Phomvihane announced new policies. There had been mistakes, he said. The government had tried to push the country toward socialism too quickly. Taxes would be reduced. Private ownership and foreign investment would be allowed once more. The state would enter into partnership with private ventures. Trade with Thailand and Western nations would be increased.

Gradually the tension in the country lessened. In 1981 self-sufficiency in rice production was announced. Stores were

The government is trying to increase the production of crops such as corn (left), rice (right), and other produce (opposite page, left).

reopened and goods returned to the marketplaces. There were fewer midnight escapes across the Mekong River to the Thai refugee camps. By 1984 some people were being allowed to travel to the United States and France to visit resettled family members. The Laotian and the United States governments completed an agreement to search for the bodies of American soldiers missing in action.

The goal of socialism with its state-controlled production and equal division of wealth has not been forgotten. Government limitations and taxes prevent anyone from accumulating too much money or property. Cooperative farming and state stores are being experimented with and improved. The destructive practice of slashing and burning the jungles to create temporary farm acreage is still forbidden. As a result, there are still forced resettlements of tribes from their homes and their traditional ways of life to new villages and new techniques in the lower lands. But changes now are made less often by force and more often with incentives and persuasion.

*People have to be careful
what they say and do because
Laos is not a democracy.*

Laos is not a democracy. People have to be very careful what they say and do. There are resistance groups in the hills and on the borders depending on cooperation within the country. The government is determined they will not succeed.

The war has left its reminders. Tiny bombs from American planes lay buried in the soil to be detonated with a swing of a hoe. Ferries are built from old United States pontoons and fences from United States bomb casings. There are very few families that did not have someone die in the war or suffer the pain of reeducation camps, prison, or escape.

The Laotian government is struggling to rebuild the economy of Laos and to regain the trust of its citizens. To succeed as a state, it must have good relations both with the Communist countries surrounding it and the Western world. The many people of Laos must overcome their differences and work together as one country.

Various tribal groups live in Laos.

Chapter 6

THE MANY PEOPLE
OF LAOS

Laos is rippled with mountains and rivers. On all its borders are stronger nations: China, Vietnam, Burma, Cambodia, and Thailand. Refugees from these states, soldiers, land-hungry farmers, and nomadic tribesmen have threaded through the mountain passes to seek shelter in Laos. Each group of people found a pocket of the mountains or a river valley to settle in. They stayed distinct in language, dress, and custom. The Lao government counts sixty-eight tribal minorities. Some have less than five thousand members.

THE LAO LUM

The Lao Lum are the most powerful segment of Lao society. They speak the official Lao language, control the government, and belong to the Buddhist religion, which is the basis for most Laotian holidays. When the Laotian people are spoken of, it is usually the Lao Lum that are meant.

The Lao Lum are often called the Lowland Lao because they make their homes by the Mekong River and its tributaries. They were originally Tai from China. Conflicts between tribal leaders and Chinese domination caused them to migrate to Laos about A.D. 700. King Khun Borom, who is given credit for the beginnings of the Lao state, was a Tai king. The wanderings of these Tai ethnic groups brought them to Laos, Thailand, northern portions of Vietnam, and as far away as northeastern India. The Laotians of Laos make up a small percentage of the world's Tai.

The Laotian-Tai language, like Chinese, is tonal. The same syllable can have an entirely different meaning depending upon the inflection. Sometimes a word will have a rising tone like the end of a question in English or a falling tone like the finish of an English statement. The number of different tones and the combination of tone and word often distinguish the dialect of one Tai group from another. In addition, the Tai vocabulary contains terms of respect; the language changes with the importance of the person being addressed.

Last names in Laos are a fairly new custom. Family names were not required until 1943. In the villages where most people knew each other, two names were not needed. The phone book, even today, is organized under first names.

LAO LUM DRESS

The Lao Lum men usually wear a pullover shirt and blue jeans. During festivals or on state occasions, the men may dress in the traditional *pa salong*. This ankle-length pair of pants shaped from a single piece of silk is wrapped around the waist, brought through the legs, and tucked in at the back.

A young girl wears a sinh (left) and a man (right) relaxes in his pa khao ma.

In the village the farmers often wear a *pa khao ma*. This wide band of cotton cloth can be folded to fit the need of the moment. On a hot day, the farmer winds it turban style around his head. In the rice paddy he wraps it like a sarong for a cool, comfortable pair of shorts. It can be a sash to hold money for the market, a warm scarf, or a towel for dusty hands.

The Lao Lum women wear the *sinh*, a homespun, softly patterned skirt of cotton or silk that falls just below the knee. It is 1 yard wide (.9 meter) and 2 yards (1.8 meters) long sewn to a border interlaced with gold or silver. The sinh is worn wrapped and tucked around the waist. A wide belt holds it in place. Above the sinh the Lao Lum women put on a solid-color blouse and sometimes use a shawl over the left shoulder.

It is common to go barefoot, especially in the village or at home. No shoes are allowed in the Buddhist temples. Both men and women wear sandals in the city.

Lao Lum homes are open and airy. The veranda is used for eating meals and entertaining guests.

LAO LUM HOMES

The Lao Lum home perches on wooden stilts 6 to 8 feet (1.8 to 2.4 meters) in the air. The stilts rise the height of the house to support a roof made of thatch, bamboo shingles, wood, or corrugated iron. The rooms are open and airy. A bamboo veranda where the family eats, washes, and entertains guests crosses the front. Inside, curtains extend the length of the house separating sleeping spaces from the family's common room. Mats are rolled out for beds. Cushions and stools take the place of chairs. Instead of nails, the walls are joined by pegs, bamboo, and rattan ties. Beneath the house, the family stores tools, weaves cloth, perhaps raises a few pigs or chickens and, if lucky, shelters a motorcycle.

The white stucco or concrete city houses are built directly on the ground. Merchants make their homes above their shops. Some houses have replaced the wind with air conditioning and the charcoal fires or kerosene burners with small electric stoves.

Laotians customarily squat or sit on the floor when they eat.

LAO LUM PATTERN OF LIFE AND RELIGION

Often in a Lao Lum kitchen the smell of hot chicken soup steams from the bowls. A paste of pounded onions, garlic, and stinging red peppers seasons the broth. Vegetables come from a garden behind the house. Sweets are made from coconut milk simmered with bananas or crisp pieces of pumpkin and sugar. At each meal every person has a small, hinged basket called a *tip kow* filled with sticky rice, which is kneaded between the fingertips and eaten like bread. The different foods are placed around a mat on the veranda where the family gathers to eat.

The pattern of the year for the Lao Lum is determined by the planting and harvesting of the sticky rice. Monsoon rains begin about May. By that time the tender green rice shoots are already poking up from the first beds. Men and oxen prepare the rice paddies. Then the trimmed carpet of small rice sprouts is rolled up and transplanted into the watery furrows of the paddy. After

Left: Boys often enter the wats as novices and receive their education there. Right: A monk stands in front of the residence he shares with the other monks.

planting and prayers for rain, the farmer is free to attend to the other chores of the village. In October all work stops again while the rice is harvested. "If you have sticky rice, you have everything. You can sell it, raise a pig, make cereal, distill rice wine, and still have food for your family all year."

As the growing of the rice plans the seasons, the Buddhist religion directs the everyday events. A village does not really exist until it builds its wat. The wat is used as a meeting place, a library for sacred texts, and as an inn to shelter travelers as well as monks. Its gongs and drums call to the people in the morning. Housewives wait along the street or before their doors with bits of rice to feed the begging monks. Perhaps a cousin or a brother is among them dressed in orange robes, with his head shaven. Boys often enter wats as novices and receive their education there. For some, being a monk is a lifetime commitment. For others, it is part of the natural process of becoming a man and involves taking a certain amount of time to separate oneself from society to pray

The interior of a wat

and serve others. The stay may be as brief as three months, but later in life a man may return to the wat for reflection and renewal.

A Buddhist monk is forbidden to destroy life, steal, lie, drink alcohol, eat except at certain times, use perfume or ornaments, sleep on high beds, or accept money. He takes a vow of poverty, owning only a yellow robe, a begging bowl, a fan, an umbrella, a bag, and some needles. He sets aside his desire for material things in order to meditate on life and serve others. The monks bless the new home, marry the young couples, treat the sick, and say prayers over the dead.

But just to make sure that life and the fields and the weather will be kind, the housewife also hurries out to the small spirit house in her garden. There she has a pinch of food to give to the tiny spirits of the phi and a quick prayer for their blessing too. Officially the Buddhist temple and the Communist government

A village water system built of bamboo, brings water from the mountains.

discourage belief in spirits. Privately, the monk says: "If you believe in phi, then, for you, they exist." Unhappy phi, perhaps the soul of someone who died a violent death, roam the forest looking for a body to enter or a stranger to torment. A person who behaves in a peculiar way is believed to be possessed by a phi and is often expelled from the village.

Most phi, however, are kind. It is their job to bless the harvest, guard the homes, and to live in and look after all the natural elements of the world.

In the Lao Lum community everyone's contribution is valued. Even small children bring water to the garden, throw grain to the chickens, and run off on errands. When rice is planted and harvested, both men and women work in the fields. Children are cared for and loved by the entire extended family. If someone is sick or a crop has failed, the whole village helps. At marriage, a man moves into the house of his wife's parents. The arrangement may be permanent if the bride is the last daughter. People work as long as they can and give advice when they are no longer able to

Children are cared for by the extended family, where age and position are held in respect.

do it themselves. Age and position are respected. Sons and daughters are always considered part of their parents' household.

THE LAO THEUNG

Living in small villages tucked into the forested hills at elevations near to or under 3,500 feet (1,067 meters) are the Lao Theung. These are not one group of people, but many small tribal communities varying in name, dress, and custom. They make up between 20 and 30 percent of the Lao population. In Lao history, the Lao Theung are mentioned as the first inhabitants of Laos, crossing over from the southern seas near Indonesia. When the strong Tai (Lao Lum) streamed down from the highlands of

Yunnan Province in China, they pushed the Lao Theung out of the river valleys into the hills. They named them Kha. Just as the Chinese had ruled over the Tai, the Tai dominated the Lao Theung. Even up to recent times, most Lao Theung had no education, no representation in the government, and none but the lowest jobs.

The largest group of Lao Theung belong to the Khmu tribe. There are also many Lamet and Loven and more than twenty other tribes with smaller populations. Despite their differences, the Lao Theung have enough in common to be considered as one division in the Laotian world.

Most of the Lao Theung live south in the Bolovens Plateau or north near the Vietnamese and Chinese borders. They speak, along with some Laotian, Mon-Khmer languages similar to that spoken in Cambodia and the Malay Peninsula. The languages have no written form.

EVERYDAY LIFE, CUSTOMS, AND RELIGION OF THE LAO THEUNG

The Lao Theung are a diverse people, generally smaller and darker than most Lao Lum. Their dress is simple, usually a version of the sarong for both men and women. Shoes are seldom worn. Sometimes over long distances, a man will carry his belongings in a pack attached to a shoulder board fastened around the neck. In the city the Lao Theung women often dress with sinhs and the men wear Western-style pants like the Laotians around them.

Lao Theung villages are in clearings cut out of the forest. The homes are long, rectangular buildings of wood and woven bamboo, each capable of housing as many as three separate families. A men's longhouse for unmarried or widowed men stands in the middle of the village. In the kitchens, pots sit on three rocks over a fire that should never go out. Vegetables and herbs hang to dry from the ceilings, their fragrance filling the rooms. The houses are open and angled to let in the cool breezes.

Simmering in the pot may be rice or a meaty stew spiced with peppers. The rice is sometimes the sweet, sticky rice of the Lao Lum, but more often it is the drier upland kind. The Lao Theung raise pigs, chickens, and some water buffalo. They hunt quail, snakes, small birds, deer, squirrels, monkeys, or rabbits in the dense surrounding forests. Patches of land near the village are cleared of trees and brush and set afire. This is called slash and burn. The ashes are used to fertilize the soil for crops of rice, corn, tobacco, and cotton. When after several years the soil wears out, the whole village simply moves to another section of the forest and begins again.

Men of the Lao Theung tribes often trade in the towns. They bring forest products: skins, benzoin used as a base for perfumes and ointments, and sticklac, an ingredient in varnish and lacquer. Some stay for a while working at odd jobs. When they return to the village, they may take back medicines, silver, cloth, water buffalo, and the gongs and metal drums that are used in religious ceremonies.

The spirits the Lao Theung worship—the Khmu call them *hrooy*—are powerful and mischievous like the phi. A spirit given the proper attention multiplies the crops and blesses the family. An angry spirit, however, scares the game from the forest, keeps the rains from the fields, and brings death and disease into the village. Sorcerers are respected for their ability to communicate with the spirit world and to direct the sacrifices of chickens or water buffalo before planting and harvest. During these times strangers are not welcome in the village. Often the position of the sorcerer is hereditary, a father passes the knowledge to his son. In addition to the spirits, ancestors are requested to return to share their wisdom and protection.

The sorcerer and the village chief hold the most respected positions in the village. The Lao Theung tribes have many different ways of naming a chief. They may choose one person or a group. The position may be hereditary, by election, or determined by wealth. Regardless, the authority of the chief is seldom all-powerful. He is considered first among equals. The chief settles disputes, helps decide when and where to move the village, and deals with officials from the government.

Since many Lao Theung seldom leave their village in the forest, tribal leaders who know of the outside world are respected. Many of the Pathet Lao guerrillas were selected from the Lao Theung villages. The Communists capitalized on their ignorance and their mistrust of the Lao Lum. They were promised education, equality, and a better life. When the men returned home, the people of the village listened to them and believed. Much of the strength of the guerrilla movement came from the Lao Theung tribes.

HMONG

The Hmong, Yao (Mien), and Man tribes are the "people of the mountain," the Lao Soung. They migrated to Laos from southern China just 150 years ago. Some groups are still in China, others traveled not to Laos, but east to the highlands of North Vietnam and south to Thailand. These people are closer in race to the

*A Meo man with his horse (left)
and a Meo mother and child (right)*

Chinese than are any other Laotians. They have been a part of
Chinese history and referred to in ancient scrolls for more than
4,000 years.

The Meo are by far the largest group of Lao Soung, estimated at
about 400,000. *Meo* in Lao means "barbarian." The tribe's own
name, *Hmong*, means "free people." They have a tradition of
independence, of strength, and of willingness to fight to maintain
their freedom. In 1919 the Hmong revolted against a harsh French
tax. This "Madman's War," as the French called it, lasted more
than two years. The fury of the resisting Hmong was strengthened
by a legend that someday a leader will arise uniting the clans into
a nation of their own. This same belief and determination to
remain independent involved the Hmong heavily in the recent
war between the Pathet Lao and the Royal Laotian government.

The majority of Hmong live in the northeastern plateau of
Xieng Khouang Province at elevations ranging from 4,000 to 9,000
feet (1,219 to 2,743 meters). Usually there is only one clan in a
village of two to forty houses. There are twenty separate Hmong

clans all together. While the Laotians distinguish the Hmong by their costumes: White Hmong, Flowered Hmong, Striped Hmong; the Hmong's own names for their clans are rooted in the mythology of a heroic ancestor who may have lived a thousand years ago. Hmong personal names are short and Chinese sounding in comparison to the longer rhythmic names of the Lao Lum. Compare the Hmong: Tou Yang or Neng Le to the Laotian: Savannikone Khathakhanthaphixay.

CUSTOMS, LANGUAGE, EVERYDAY LIFE, AND RELIGION OF THE HMONG

In most cases, the oldest householder in the village is automatically chief. His word is absolute. He makes village decisions, administers justice, and interacts with the Hmong provincial officials. Up until his death in 1975, the Laotian government recognized Touby Lyfong as the paramount chief of all Hmong. He was the first Hmong to hold a position, the minister of health, in the national government. A similar status has been given by the Pathet Lao to another chieftain, Faydang Lobliayao.

When a woman marries, she keeps her clan name. Her home, however, is in her husband's village. All her children belong to her husband's clan and may not marry within it.

Before marriage, a suitor must get permission of the girl's parents and give them a bride price. Polygamy is common. This is especially true now since so many men have been killed during the war. If a man dies, custom demands that his brother marry and care for his wife.

The language of the Hmong and the other Lao Soung tribes is

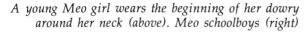
A young Meo girl wears the beginning of her dowry around her neck (above). Meo schoolboys (right)

Meo-Yao. It is similar to Chinese in form, although not in vocabulary. Like the other languages of Laos, it is tonal with seven higher or lower tones giving different meanings to the same sounds. Meo-Yao is a soft language with no final consonants.

Usually both Hmong men and women wear a loose, black, pajama-type shirt and pants. The Hmong woman's formal costume represents her skill and the wealth of her family. Each girl must sew and embroider a heavy pleated skirt that may be twenty feet (six meters) wide at the hem. It is dark with sharp accents of color along the apron and in the sash. Every clan has its traditional design. On her head, the girl wears her clan's headdress tufted with yarn or striped with colored bands. Around her neck, she carries necklaces of rounded silver bars, chains, and bangles. Her beauty, her skill at sewing and weaving, and the prestige of her household are all displayed in her costume.

Young girl models the formal costume of Hmong women.

including oranges, papayas, peaches, apples, and pineapples. Most households have a pig, a few chickens, perhaps a goat, and several water buffalo. Most Hmong families have a horse. There is a great deal of pride in these small, agile horses and in the Hmong's ability to ride them.

The most famous crop of the Hmong farmers, however, is the drug opium. It has brought them prosperity, and prosperity has brought the Hmong respect among the other tribes. Despite world opinion against opium, the French, the Royal Laotian government, and the Communists, as well as the Hmong, have all profited by it.

The Hmong create their fields by burning the forest just as the Lao Theung do. This operation of slash and burn has destroyed

Village children take a ride on a water buffalo.

almost 400 square miles (1,036 square kilometers) of trees each year. Experts suggest that, unless it is stopped, all forests may be gone from Laos in a century. The Communists have forbidden the practice, but traditions of generations are slow to change.

Finding a new location for a village is done with great care. The soil must taste sweet indicating a high lime content for the opium. It must be possible to place the house with the ordinary door opening east and the ceremonial door facing down the mountain. Since as many as thirty-five people may sleep in one building or several buildings clustered closely together, there must be space. Once the site is chosen, the Hmong house is different from any other in Laos. It is built entirely out of wood hewn with an axe. It sits directly on the ground unlike the stilted houses of the Lao Lum and the Lao Theung. There is a sleeping room and a common room. In one corner, an altar is recessed in the wall. There are no windows, just cracks and the two doors to let in light. A fireplace for cooking and daily needs is at one end of the house. A fireplace for family gatherings and guests is at the other end.

A group of Meo houses in a clearing in the mountains

Food in Hmong households is generally steamed upland rice and boiled vegetables. Sometimes meat from chicken, pork, or game is added. The variety, as with Chinese food, lies in the seasonings. No milk, cheese, or eggs are eaten.

The roaming spirits that are worshiped under so many names in Laos live with the Hmong also. Here they are called *tlan* and are souls of ancestors from generations past. Like the phi of the Lao Lum or the hrooy of the Lao Theung, they can be either kind or jealous and dangerous. In each village, a chosen person understands and communicates with the spirits.

The war between the Communists and the Royal Lao government tore the Hmong from their traditional patterns of life. Even before the fighting reached the mountains, other arguments had split the clans. The faction headed by Faydang Lobliayao distrusted the French and all the Western powers associated with them. He and his group fought for the Pathet Lao. Touby Lyfong and his general, Vang Pao, formed an opposing force. These Hmong began by rescuing American pilots bailing out over the mountains. Eventually they formed such a vital part of the pro-Western forces that the CIA paid them directly, bypassing the Lao government completely. Hmong men turned from farmers to soldiers. Many left the mountains for the city. At one time during the war, 80 percent of the taxi drivers in Vientiane were Hmong.

In 1975 the Pathet Lao Communists won the war. Thousands of Hmong were airlifted in the bellies of American troop planes to resettle as refugees in the United States. Remaining Hmong grouped in guerrilla bands and struck at the new Communist government from the mountaintops. The Communists were savage in their retaliation. Families and villages trying to escape were showered with waves of napalm gas and bombs from Russian and captured American planes. The Hmong had no defense. Hundreds, old and young, soldiers and children alike, were killed. It is believed that now there are only 100,000 Hmong left in Laos. Some are still strong supporters of the Communist government. Some Hmong still fight. Most are simply trying to rebuild their villages and their lives.

TRIBAL DIFFERENCES

The terms Lao Lum, Lao Theung, and Lao Soung are as much descriptions of where the tribes live as they are descriptions of the tribes themselves. The Lao Lum are from the lowlands; the Lao Theung from the hills; and the Lao Soung from the mountaintops. Although within these groups there are many similarities, there are also many differences. Tribes living fifteen miles (twenty-four kilometers) of each other may not share the same language or customs. It is the challenge of the new government to take the sixty-eight ethnic minorities and to make one nation of them.

Chapter 7

DIFFERENT WAYS
OF LEARNING

TRADITIONAL EDUCATION

"Treat him as you see fit provided you return his eyes and bones." With these traditional words the Laotian father placed his son in the hands of the monks. The ten-year-old boy would now live in the wat as a novice. If it were a larger wat, he would learn teachings of Buddha, the Lao language, moral laws, some biology, history, geography, and arithmetic. A novice also learned calligraphy and Pali, a sacred, religious language, so that he would be able to make graceful copies of the ancient books. Smaller wats taught less, according to the knowledge of the monks who lived in them.

FRENCH PUBLIC SCHOOLS

When the French expanded their control of Indochina to Laos, public schools similar to those in France were established. At first they were small. In 1930 there were only seven thousand students in a country of three million people. But by World War II, the

Opposite page: A statue of a sitting Buddha greets visitors to this hillside temple in Luang Prabang.

It is now obligatory for children to attend school from age six to fourteen.

number had grown to fifteen thousand, including some special schools. Silversmiths trained at Khong, weavers at Pakse, and woodworkers at Vientiane. A few girls gradually joined their brothers in classes.

The census in 1970 counted 200,000 students at public schools and many others still being educated in the wats. The same census reported a literacy rate of 60 percent among men and just over 20 percent among women. A law had been passed ordering children six to fourteen to be in school. But in a country of many mountains and scattered settlements, it was a law difficult to enforce. City children, generally Lao Lum, went to the French-style schools. Most others did not. The Chinese- and English-speaking foreigners organized their own classes and learned in their own languages. The Laotian government claimed in 1971 that one thousand students had graduated that year, each having completed thirteen years of education. Many of these went to France to finish their studies at a university. Those wishing to stay in Laos were able to study law, education, medicine, or agriculture in Vientiane. There was also a choice of two technical schools with courses in metals, mechanics, electricity, and construction.

OVERCOMING ILLITERACY

The Pathet Lao took control in 1975, determined to wipe out illiteracy. Teachers were sent into the farthest villages. Special classes were begun for adults. By 1985, the Communists maintained they had doubled the literacy rate with over 80 percent of the population now able to read.

In the cities, books and the government newspaper are available. Some books are printed in Laos, others are brought from Thailand, which has a language almost identical to Lao. Then there are imported, foreign books from Russia, China, and Vietnam. The villages, however, have almost no printed material except the religious texts in the wat. A person learns to read and is listed in government statistics as literate. Without books and with time, the skill fades.

School in Laos during the period of the Royal Laotian government began when the child was six years old. Elementary education was divided into two sections of three years each. Middle school lasted four years, and it took three more years to complete high school. Children attended school six days a week. Their day began at 8:00 A.M. As is usual in tropical countries, the fierce noonday sun compelled a break of at least two hours, usually 11:00 A.M. until 1:00 P.M. Afternoon studies then resumed from 1:00 P.M. until 5:00 P.M. Saturday classes were held only in the morning.

Teaching was usually done by lecture rather than discussion or independent study. Situations where students' lack of knowledge might embarrass them were avoided. For this reason and in order not to bother a busy teacher, students often turned to each other for help.

Only one out of ten primary students becomes eligible to enter secondary levels.

Each year a test determined whether a student could pass to the next level. It was not unusual to spend two years in one grade. Another competitive examination was held to enter high school. Whether from lack of desire, need at home, or failure to pass the test, only one out of ten primary students entered the secondary levels. At the end of high school, a final exam developed by the government was given in order to graduate. This exam was administered twice a year and could be repeated if failed.

Classes in elementary school were taught in Lao, even in areas where Lao was not the native language. French instruction began in the fourth grade and another language was required by the seventh. High school students took exams to decide if they would specialize in literature, science, mathematics, or economics. High school was conducted completely in French. Lao was treated as a foreign language. French history and culture were required courses. Many of the graduates complain even now that they know more about France than they know about their own country.

One of the first changes of the new Communist government was to require that classes from elementary through university levels be taught in Lao. Any foreign teacher was paired with a Lao interpreter. Lao history and geography were emphasized over French history and geography. Languages were still available: French, English, Russian, and Spanish, but only one or two hours a week instead of every day. The French system of yearly examinations also was dropped. Student failure or success was now based on daily grades. Because of the many teachers that had fled the country and because of the increase in schools, there was a tremendous teacher shortage. Sometimes, especially in elementary levels, being able to read was the only requirement for teaching school.

Now classes still start at 8:00 in the morning as in the old system, but in many schools the day begins with an hour of political discussion. A leader is chosen for each seven to ten students based on academic ability and belief in the new policies of the government. The leader is supposed to guide the other students on the team.

PRACTICAL LEARNING

Practical learning is considered just as important as book learning. People are expected to work with their hands as well as their head. Everyone must contribute something. Each day for a few hours after lunch, the students spend time in the school gardens. Saturday is called *Red Saturday* and, instead of studying, the students are required to donate free labor to the school farm or wherever else they are wanted. Laos needs to educate workers quickly and put them back into the economy.

Left: People bathing in the polluted waters of the Mekong River
Right: A mother and her daughter await their turn
at a health clinic.

HEALTH CARE

Another emphasis of the government is training health-care workers to go into the villages. One out of four children die before they are five. Tuberculosis, dengue fever, the skin sores of yaws, typhoid fever, malaria, pneumonia, and parasites are all common. Many of these diseases are easily cured with modern medicines. Often, however, medicines are not available and, when they are, there are not enough people able to administer them.

The Mekong and its streams are used for transportation, watering animals, bathing, and clearing the wastes of the land, as well as for drinking. So most drinking water is polluted. Disease-carrying mosquitoes and other insects swarm by the warm, humid riverbanks. The Lowland Lao have developed an immunity to many of the tropical diseases. But when the Hmong or Lao Theung settle in lower areas, sickness spreads through whole villages.

Laotians believe that not only germs and viruses cause disease, but also unfriendly phi, the power of a distant sorcerer, or the abandonment of one or more of the body's thirty-two souls. The first remedies a Laotian tries are *hak mai*, medicines developed by the monks from the roots, leaves, and flowers of plants. These cures from the forest can be quite effective. Modern medicines sometimes come from research into these traditional treatments.

Often the family will visit a Chinese herbal pharmacy. Boxes and boxes of sweet- and bitter-smelling herbs, the result of generations of collection and study, fill the shelves of the shop. A dried leaf or root can be laid against a sore skin, boiled into a tea, or sniffed by a stuffed nose.

To increase the power of the medicines, the Lao Lum may have a *baci*, or a community prayer celebration. In the mountains, the Hmong call wise men who go into a trance in order to communicate with the evil spirits causing the disease. Each clan has its own rituals that weave together faith and hope for a cure.

The Communists' priority on educating health-care workers to combat these problems of disease and malnutrition has helped. By 1977 they claimed to have trained more than 6,000 health-care cadres. There is supposed to be a hospital in each of the 112 district towns, plus 16 province hospitals for a total of 8,970 beds. Before 1976, they said, there was one doctor for 35,000 people. Now they count one doctor or doctor's assistant for every 2,000 people. However good this sounds on paper, Laos's medical problems are not solved. Many health-care workers get only a few weeks training. Some doctors leave school with three years of education instead of the usual six. A hospital may be just a simple hut with a few beds and little more than aspirin to prescribe. Nevertheless the problems have been recognized and efforts are underway to try to treat them.

Chapter 8

LAOS AND LEISURE

CELEBRATIONS

In September, when Buddhist Lent is over and the monks return to village life, the whole country gets ready for a celebration called *boun*. A traveling troupe of actors may perform traditional love stories or transform some local news into comedy or drama. In the fields, wagers are placed on prize roosters preening and strutting before their afternoon's fight.

The men of the village set up their own contests, verbal battles, or debates. Which is better: a fat wife or a thin wife, village life or city life? The outcome is not as important to the audience as the style and flash of the argument.

Fortunes are told about the future. Not many admit to believing, but the possibility brings the curious to try. A hollow bamboo piece is filled with numbered sticks from one to ninety-nine. If it is shaken hard, a stick will drop out. The stick's number matches a prediction printed on a poster tacked to a tree.

Nearby a stone Buddha sits. People whisper a wish or try to lift the Buddha. If the Buddha can be lifted, the wish will be granted. It is said sometimes a child can lift it when a grown man cannot.

Later, broken dreams, fulfilled wishes, and naughty tricks are spun into long, involved tales by a storyteller.

Opposite page: Buddha plays an important part in all Laotian celebrations.

Villagers enjoying a feast

FOOD

Celebrations are a time to feast. Chickens are skewered and roasted slowly over a pit of glowing branches. Platters of a meat dish called *lab,* meaning "good luck," are served. It has been ground and sharply spiced. Not quite ripe papayas are mashed with tomatoes, limes, garlic, and red hot peppers for a salad that stings the taste buds. The children love to eat sweet bamboo sticks. These have been stuffed with sticky rice, red beans, coconut milk, and sugar, and then cooked slowly in hot ashes. It takes just a few moments to peel the green bamboo off, uncovering the sweet, crunchy rice cylinder.

MUSIC AND DANCE

Late in the afternoon, the musicians gather. The tunes from the *khene,* a tall Laotian flute, spread out into the warm evening air.

Left: A musician plays a traditional bamboo horn called a kreong.
Right: Mothers tuck their babies into the shawls they wear on their backs.

The music is soft and high and slightly Chinese. It has taken a
long apprenticeship to learn to lash the four to sixteen bamboo
canes into an instrument and to pull the notes from their many
mouths. In the background, a two-stringed violin, a xylophone,
and cymbals attached to a curved frame of wood play in gentle
accompaniment. Women dance the *lamvong* on stage, lightly
touching bare feet to the wooden boards and weaving stories with
their arms and fingertips. They circle each other gracefully, never
touching. It is almost dark when the last notes die away. The
mothers tuck their babies into the shawls on their backs and
gather their children. Small groups of people stop for a last joke or
a bit of discussion before climbing the stairs of the houses on
stilts. The village becomes quiet.

The Laotians love leisure. There are fifteen religious festivals a
year. The most common unscheduled festival is the baci.

A sleeping baby wears cotton threads around his wrists, from the baci festival, to bring him good luck.

THE BACI FESTIVAL

A baci is held for the birth of a baby, a new mother, someone just recovered from an illness, a person about to leave on a long journey, or one just returning. The invited guests sit in a circle around a small shrine made of banana leaves and flowers. Foods such as boiled chicken, eggs, and cakes ring the centerpiece. These symbolize the wish for freedom from hunger. The host greets the honored guest with poetry and prayers to welcome and wish him or her good fortune. The wandering souls of the company are called to come back and watch over them. Every person is said to have thirty-two souls, protecting each part of the body. The lesser ones stay at the feet and the most important at the head. This is why it is considered very rude to touch someone's head or sit with the feet pointing out. The baci concludes with more prayers and with cotton threads tied around the guest's wrists symbolizing the uniting of the souls with the body.

NEW YEAR'S CELEBRATION

New Year's is probably the biggest celebration. It should fall in December, but that is not considered a fortunate time by astrologers. April is chosen instead. It is a month of more light—thus more good fortune. It is also the beginning of the rainy season, a time to plant the rice that will feed Laos in the coming year. The New Year's festival lasts three days. On April 15 every member of the family lights four candles, each one the length of a part of their body. These symbolize the offering of the body to Buddha. During this day, everyone cleans his house and helps to scrub the statues at the village wat. Houses and wats are decorated with waving bands of colored paper. They are covered with figures from the Chinese twelve-year zodiac: the Rat, the Ox, the Tiger, the Hare, the Dragon, the Snake, the Horse, the Ram, the Monkey, the Rooster, the Dog, and the Pig. Sand shrines are built in the wat's courtyard and planted with flags, flowers, and money. Engaged couples share the building of one shrine to show togetherness.

The second day is dangerous. The old year has left but the goddess of the new year has not come yet. People douse each other with water, washing away the past. It can get quite wild, but nobody seems to mind.

On the last day, children ask a yearly forgiveness from their parents. In the city of Luang Prabang, people buy fish and birds to release in the evening illustrating Buddha's compassion for animals. The New Year is supposed to begin at exactly thirty seconds after 7:50 P.M. on the last evening and is brought in by baci, dancing, and celebration.

Pedicab passengers (left) and a girl on a bicycle (right)
get doused with water on the second day of the New Year's celebration.

OTHER HOLIDAYS

Among other holidays, Boum Bam Fay in May celebrates Buddha's birth, enlightenment, and death. It is combined with a more ancient ceremony demanding rain from the gods. All the villages and wats compete in constructing and firing elaborate, many-colored rockets.

There is also a holiday for the beginning of Buddhist Lent in July as the monks prepare to go into seclusion for three months. Another holiday celebrates the end of Lent in September.

In October or November, Luang Prabang has its famous boat races. People come from every part of Laos to the city to watch the long, sleek boats race in the Mekong.

LEISURE

In between all the holidays, if the weather is kind and the war is far away, there is time to combine play with work. Boys follow

The main market in Vientiane

their fathers into the fields, girls weave in the coolness under the houses with their mothers. Sometimes, during the dry season, whole villages take the day to go fishing.

In the cities the streets are filled with each day's shopping for dinner, gossip, and laughter. On market days, everyone is in town. Perhaps a honey seller has golden streams of honey to pour into bottles from home, or belts or bicycles have arrived from Thailand or Vietnam.

In the afternoon or at night, borders and politics cannot stop television programs broadcasting from Thailand and propaganda films sent from Vietnam to cities and towns with electricity. Movie houses on the main streets lure customers into another strange, more romantic world. Before the Communists arrived in 1975, twenty-foot (six-meter) tall signs burst from the top of the theaters advertising adventures from Thailand or America. Now posters are simpler and the movies come from Russia or Eastern Europe, but the lines of eager customers are still there.

Song, story, play, and sport are not separated from life in Laos; they are a part of it. Most amusements are not imported but created by a neighbor in the village or town. The sinhs are woven by mothers and daughters at their own looms. The silver maker, the storyteller, and the dancers of the lamvong are neighbors and friends. Soccer games are not played in amphitheaters by professionals, but are matches set up between towns or just between teams picked randomly on a village field. In Laos the arts belong to everyone, inseparably interwoven with daily life.

SPORTS AND GAMES

Finished with work or school, the young men and the children play games. Soccer and volleyball are popular and so is a highly skilled combination of the two called *ga to*. Three or more people stand on each side of a net trying to keep a tightly wound ball of rattan straw in the air. No hands are allowed. The ball can be slammed with the feet or bounced off the head or shoulder. Sometimes a particularly limber player will somersault and kick the ball as he flips.

The children play with dolls, balls, and make tracks in the dust with toy cars like children everywhere. Jump ropes are often loops of rubber bands tied together. Marbles grow on trees. A huge seed pod, 3 feet (.9 meters) or more long, provides round, half-inch (.15-meter) seeds. The children pop the seeds out and aim them at a hole punched in the ground with a stick. Small toys are always for sale in the markets and wealthier families buy imported games or dolls.

Some Laotian handicrafts include woven baskets (above), carved silver jewelry (left), and brightly patterned cloth (far left).

HANDICRAFTS

Not everything in the state stores and markets is practical. In each part of Laos, there are handicrafts whose distinct patterns identify the place and people who made them. Baskets of bamboo or straw in all sizes are brought from the villages to sell. Thick yarn shopping bags just big enough to carry a morning's groceries from town are interwoven with color. Silkworms feed on mulberry leaves and flax grows in the fields to provide thread, which is woven into brightly patterned cloth. The style, design, and color of the cloth is individual for each separate clan in Laos. From certain towns around Luang Prabang and from the Hmong clans, gold and silver are worked into jewelry and dishes.

The Hmong women are expert seamstresses. They cut and sew

A sleeping Buddha carved of stone

bits of cloth to make wall hangings and tablecloths. These are called *pandau* in the Hmong language, meaning "to cut cloth like flowers." The hangings may be geometric designs of diamonds, circles, and spirals repeated over and over. Frequently they are scenes remembered from folk stories, a soldier firing a gun or a downed plane joins the cutouts of paths, trees, and animals of the forest or village.

RELIGIOUS ART

Many crafts and pieces of art are created for religious purposes. Small Buddhas are carved from ivory or wood to be worn around the neck or sit protectively in someone's home. Larger Buddhas, some as tall as eighteen feet (five meters), are chiseled from stone or formed from bronze to join centuries-old copies in temples or caves. The Buddhas smile serenely as they walk, sit, or lie in traditional styles brought from India a thousand years before.

Temple mosaic representing a sheep

The Emerald Buddha, carved from flowing green jasper, is said to have special powers. It was made in India just over two thousand years ago. When invaders attacked the city where it sat, it was hurried off to another Buddhist capital. The Emerald Buddha traveled from India to Ceylon, to Burma, to Cambodia, and finally to an ancient kingdom of Laos. It was disguised by painting it with a coat of lacquer and lime and hiding it in a village temple. In 1434, lightning struck the Buddha revealing the precious green jasper. For four hundred years, it sat in honored splendor in Laos. Then Thai troops attacked in 1780, capturing the country and the statue. The conquering army carried the Emerald Buddha off to Thailand and it is still there, as monks teach every Laotian child, waiting for Laos to reclaim it.

Religious art is not just in the Buddhas, but in the temples that hold them and the shrines that honor them. The edges of the temple roofs stretch out and curl upward with dragon heads on their tips. Doors hold lifelike and fanciful animals lying below

Intricately decorated temple doors

legendary heroes that they symbolize. Swirling over and between the animals and men, flowers and leaves fill in every available space. Unlike the temples, the shrines in Laos have no monks living in them. They have been erected to guard a piece of Buddha's hair, a writing, or a religious symbol. Perhaps the most famous is the That Luang in Vientiane, which has been built and rebuilt several times over the centuries so that it holds the stones of many eras. The people of Vientiane have set aside special times to honor the shrine, stringing it with colored lights and decorating it with flowers and flags from many countries.

The That Luang in Vientiane

LITERATURE

Written literature in Laos is enclosed in the temple libraries. Most texts are Buddhist, brought from India. The *Tripitaka* are sermons of Buddha written in the ancient Indian language of Pali, which all monks must learn. The *Jatakam* is a collection of 550 stories of Buddha's past lives; some serious, some funny, some satirical. Written prayers are in poetry. The spell of the words and the rhyme is thought to have a magical effect on evil spirits. Most tales in Laos, however, are not written, but told, handed down from parent to child. These adventures have brave heroes or heroines in danger and come complete with ferocious monsters and rescuing gods.

There are few historical accounts of Laos written before the French arrival in the late 1800s. Many official records were destroyed in the fires of the wars with Thailand. The best-known history still existing is *Nithane Khun Borom*, which begins with the founding of Lan Xang by the wandering King Khun Borom and continues until the end of the sixteenth century.

Above: Meo farmers working in the fields
Below: The Nam Khan River

Chapter 9

THE ECONOMY

AND THE FUTURE

RESOURCES

Laos is a country of undeveloped promise. Because of mountains, only 20,000 square miles (51,800 square kilometers) can be used for agriculture. Laos uses less than 7,000 (18,130).

There are dense forests and valleys thickly blanketed with jungle. But exports of forest products have fallen by half since 1980. Hundreds of acres of forestland have been destroyed by slash and burn farming.

Hidden beneath the rocks and streams are deposits of tin, iron, coal, lead, copper, gold, silver, phosphate, sulfur, and perhaps oil. The tin mine in Khammouan Province started by the French is struggling to begin exporting again. Most other mineral deposits are unexplored.

Rivers crash through the rocks and cascade over steep mountain drops. The possibility for hydroelectric power is enormous. Laos has only one major dam. Nam Ngum Dam near Vientiane could produce 18,000 megawatts of electricity. It produced 113 megawatts in the early 1980s. Eighty to 90 percent of that electricity was exported over high tension lines to Thailand.

The terrain in Laos makes road building expensive and difficult. Small airfields are much more practical. In 1983, Laos had only fourteen Russian aircraft, three helicopters, and maintenance problems.

SELF-SUFFICIENCY UNTIL THE 1960s

Until the fighting gathered strength in the 1960s, Laos was self-sufficient. People were able to meet their own economic needs. The women wove cotton and flax on their looms for cloth. Silkworms spun cocoons of silk used to make sinhs and shawls. The forests supplied bamboo, rattan, and wood for housing. There was plentiful wild game to hunt among the grasses of the plains and the jungles. Monsoons filled the rivers with water for the rice paddies. Water buffalo in every village tilled the furrows. Land was abundant and rich; the weather was gentle and warm. Life was not easy, but people believed in the Buddhist tradition of simplicity. There was enough.

The French never realized as much profit from Laos as they did from Vietnam. The Laotians were not much interested in imported goods, and the French did not take the time or money to develop exports.

WARS

After World War II, there was a new national consciousness in Laos and the desire to be a free state grew. Guerrilla groups gathered in each of the countries of the Indochinese Peninsula. Soon Vietnam burned with revolution, sweeping up the other countries with it.

*A Meo refugee
and his baby*

Laos was torn with war. It was no longer self-sufficient. Rice, clothing, food, and war materials were imported. In 1968 Laos imported almost fifteen times as many goods as it exported. The United States supplied $50 million in economic aid and $300 million in military aid. There were cases, as with the Hmong, where the soldiers were paid directly by the United States government. Some generals and officials built villas and bought expensive cars. There was always work in the city or the army for young men tired of farming. The economy floated on a balloon of war and foreign aid, anchored less and less to the traditional, local ways of production.

INFLATION

When the war ended, the Americans left. Within a few months all the aid was gone. Thousands of families frightened by the change of government tried to escape. In the closing days of the war, the Americans lifted many refugees by plane, others were smuggled by boat, or swam the Mekong at night. In April of 1983 it was estimated that 300,000 to 400,000 Laotians had left. The administrative base of Laos had been reduced by 80 percent. Officials, police, and soldiers who had not escaped were sent to reeducation camps, removing hundreds more educated people from society. Guerrilla bands roamed the hills and small, hostile armies of exiles regrouped on the Thai border. The Communists could claim victory in the war, but there was no peace or economic stability.

Prices rose. There were food shortages, clothing shortages, and gasoline shortages. Cars disappeared from the streets. Stores were boarded and closed. The government put strict controls on prices and wages. A shopkeeper could be arrested amd jailed for overcharging. Sometimes, without warning, soldiers would fill a shop, confiscate the goods, and transfer the store to the ownership of the state. The lines at state stores were long and the supplies were limited, but everything was cheap. Rice, which on the open market might be thirty-eight cents a kilogram (2.2 pounds), was only three cents a kilogram in the state-run store. However, a person might wait in line hours only to find, at the end, that the supply had run out.

NEW WAYS OF WORKING ENFORCED

In the villages solidarity teams were formed. Traditional cooperation of neighbors supporting neighbors became an organized, required activity. Formal labor exchanges were encouraged between towns. Contributions of work hours and loans of water buffalo were tallied supposedly to be repaid equally.

Many Hmong and Lao Theung were moved from the mountains to lower ground. Slash and burn farming was forbidden. The mountain tribes were shown new agriculture techniques and were required to use them. Methods, advisers, and fertilizers came from Vietnam.

In political meetings, the leaders explained and compared the new and the old ways. In the past, there was private production where each family might own and work plots as small as five acres (two hectares). Now the state and the farmers were a team. The goal was to create collective farms where all the land was joined together and worked together. In some provinces, the leaders tried hard to turn this goal into reality. Farm ownership was reorganized with or without the permission of the farmers. Four years after the war, one out of five farm families was involved in cooperative farming.

TAXES

Laos would have had difficulty taking care of its population after all the years of fighting even without trying so many new economic ideas. It takes time before the success or failure of changes in the economy can be measured. The Laotian government needed money immediately. A tax was imposed on land. The more land a family owned, the heavier the tax. Laotian farmers had never before experienced such taxes or such strong efforts to collect them, even in the previously controlled Communist provinces. Refugees poured out of the country. The farmers that were left destroyed their crops and killed their livestock rather than pay the taxes.

The Mekong River during the rainy season (left) and during a drought (right)

DROUGHT AND FLOODS

The economy suffered not only from human conflict, but also from the unpredictability of nature. In 1977 the rains did not come. In 1979 and 1980 there were floods. Without the regular pattern of monsoons, the rice will not grow. Fourteen percent of the population had left the country by the middle of 1979. The Laotian government asked for help.

OTHER COUNTRIES AID LAOS

Vietnam had aided the Communists for decades, starting with the first groups of Communist guerrillas. Now each of the sixteen provinces in Laos were matched with a province in Vietnam. The Vietnamese were to help their Laotian counterparts as an older brother would help a younger brother. Teams arrived from Vietnam to give advice in agriculture and to build bridges, health clinics, and schools. Laotian students were invited to study in Vietnamese cities. The Laotian government was given interest-free loans. But Vietnam was still hurting from its own war.

Vietnamese troops were battling the Chinese on the country's borders and fighting against the government in Cambodia. Ther was a limit to the help Vietnam could give Laos.

More economic aid came from the U.S.S.R. and Eastern Europe. Soviet advisers arrived although in lesser numbers than did the Vietnamese. There were study programs in the Soviet Union, and the Laotian government depended heavily on the Soviets for advice.

Sweden, Cuba, Japan, The Netherlands, Australia, and India each supplied foreign aid. Along with money, the countries donated individual projects such as the hydroelectric turbine given by Japan for the Nam Ngum Dam. International organizations including the Asian Development Bank and the United Nations Development Program started pilot farms, did research, helped with irrigation, plant construction, and veterinary medicine. The United States contributed 10,000 tons (9,072,000 kilograms) of grain in 1980 and $100,000 of medical supplies in 1981. Congress, however, had passed regulations forbidding the American government to approve additional aid for Communist Laos. It was not until 1986 that President Reagan repealed the law.

Faced with a fleeing population, a struggling economy, and dependence once again on other countries, the Laotian government debated solutions. Former government officials slowly began to be released from the reeducation camps. Their skills were needed. Many were offered jobs in administration. Bitter and wary after their years in the camps, most of the returnees avoided the offers and tried to leave Laos as soon as they were able.

AN EASING UP ON RESTRICTIONS

Both Vietnam and the U.S.S.R. advised easing up on change and loosening economic restrictions. Cooperative farming was no longer to be forced on the villages. The cooperatives collapsed. Taxes were reduced and salaries increased. Private investment was promoted. A three-year tax exemption was given to small private industries. Stores were reopened. Consumer goods and food began to fill the markets once again. Trade between provinces was allowed and trade with Thailand was encouraged.

THE ECONOMY STRENGTHENS

With borders so close, even in the most tense times, informal trade between Laos and Thailand had never really stopped. Now that the Laotians were eager to increase contact, the Thai government was hesitant. The Thai were afraid of the strengthening Laotian economy. They felt that Vietnam and the other Communist countries of the Indochinese Peninsula were just waiting for the opportunity to extend their control over Thailand as well. Three times since 1975, Thailand declared an economic boycott against Laos. Now with trade growing, there were still long lists of strategic items that the Thai refused to export including needles, thread, bikes, and medicine. Once, a shipment of asphalt bought by Japan for Laos was stopped for fear it might be used to build airplane runways. Nevertheless, today Thailand is both one of the principal exporters to Laos and an importer of Laotian goods and electricity.

Before the war, Laos exported forest products: animal hides, teak, mahogany, rosewood, sticklac, and benzoin. Food and drink also were exported, principally maize, sweet potatoes, bananas, tangerines, peanuts, coconuts, soybeans, and coffee, tea, and tobacco from the Bolovens Plateau. Lead and tin were brought up from the mines. Opium, legally or illegally, was another export.

At the present, the most profitable Laotian product is the electricity from the Nam Ngum River Dam. Timber, coffee, tea, peanuts, and soybean sales have slowly increased. Tin is once again being mined and sold; and opium is still grown in the mountain fields of the Hmong.

THE FUTURE

What is the future of Laos? The guerrilla leaders that fought and hid in the jungles for thirty years are growing old now. Many already have died. The control of the government and the management of the country will pass to younger hands.

The Communist philosophy of ownership by group rather than individual, and tight supervision over private citizens has been relaxed once. Will the Laotian government follow the lead of their advisers in the Soviet Union continuing to loosen restrictions and encouraging private farms and shops? Successful private ownership with a rich elite is against Communist beliefs. There are signs that the pull is in the opposite direction toward more traditional Communist policies. However, there have been disagreements in the government that have reached public ears. Some of these disagreements have been over management of the economy. Which ideas, or perhaps compromise between many, will finally determine the direction of the country?

How will Vietnamese control affect Laos? Will Laos, Cambodia, and Vietnam eventually be combined into one state?

There are twenty-two million Vietnamese and three million Laotians. Will the Vietnamese expand into Laos as the Tai did a thousand years ago? There are already many Vietnamese in the border towns.

What will happen to Thailand? Will the pressures of the surrounding Communist governments and Thailand's own guerrillas force that country to become Communist also?

What about the resistance groups still operating on the borders and within Laos? They have fought for more than ten years now. They can weaken the Laotian government. Will they ever be strong enough to change it?

These questions and more are debated among the thousands of Laotian refugees throughout the world and among foreign relations experts in departments of state. Whatever the answers, it does not seem that the peace, stability, and tradition of the Laotian village will soon return.

Cosmopolitan World Atlas, © Copyright 1989 by Rand McNally & Company,
R.L. 89-S-72

MAP KEY

Attapu	E7	Muang Ou Nua	A4
Bia (mountain)	C5	Muang Ou Tai	A4
Bolovens, Plateau des	E7	Muang Pakxan	C5
Chaîne Annamitique		Muang Sing	B4
(Annamite Mountains)	C6, D6, D7	Muang Souy	C5
Kading (river)	C6, D6	Muang Xaignabouri	C4
Kong (river)	E7	Muang Xepon	D7
Loi (mountain)	B5	Nape	C6
Louang Namtha	B4	Ou (river)	A4, A5, B5
Louangphrabang (Luang Prabang)	C5	Pakxe (Pakse)	E6
Mekong (river)	C4, B5, C5,	Phongsali	B5
	D4, D5, D6,	Saravan	E7
	E6, F6, F7,	Savannakhet	D6
Muang Khammouan	D6	Tranninh, Plateau du	C5
Muang Khongxedon	E6	Vientiane	D5
Muang Lan	C6	Xam Nua	B5
		Xiangkhoang	C5

119

MINI-FACTS AT A GLANCE

GENERAL INFORMATION

Official Name: Lao People's Democratic Republic

Capital: Vientiane

Official Language: Lao; French and English also are spoken

Government: Laos is a people's democratic republic with executive power in the hands of the premier. The monarchy was abolished in 1975. The government is headed by a president, who is also chairman of the Supreme People's Council, a legislative body. The secretary general of the Lao People's Revolutionary party serves as prime minister.

The country is divided into 20 provinces, each subdivided into districts, which in turn are subdivided into towns and villages.

National Song: "Pheng Sat" ("National Music")

Flag: A red band is at the top and bottom with a larger blue band between them, on which is centered a large white circle.

Money: The unit of exchange is the kip. In 1987, 35 kip were equal to one U.S. dollar.

Weights and Measures: All weights and measures are based on the metric system, except gold and silver, which are measured in bath (15 grams) or taels (30 to 35 grams).

Population: Estimated 1988 population—3,800,000; 84 percent rural, 16 percent urban

Major Cities:
Vientiane	120,000 (1984 estimate)
Pakse	37,000 (1970 estimate)
Savannakhet	35,682 (1987 estimate)
Luang Prabang	25,000 (1970 estimate)

Religion: About 95 percent of the people adhere to Therevada Buddhism. Animism is practiced among the Lao Theng, and 1.5 percent are Christian. Mahayana Buddhism and Confucianism are observed by Chinese and Vietnamese minorities.

GEOGRAPHY

Highest point: Mount Bia, 9,242 ft. (2,817 m)

Lowest Point: 594 ft. (181 m)

Mountains: The Annamite Mountains, a mountain range rising to heights of about 8,900 ft. (2,713 m), constitutes Laos's boundary with Vietnam. More than 90 percent of the land is more than 600 ft. (183 m) above sea level. The only lowlands are along the Mekong River to the west.

Rivers: The Mekong River forms the country's western boundary for the greater part of its length. It flows through the country for 300 mi. (483 km) of its course.

Climate: The climate is monsoonal; heavy rains occur from May through September and then taper off, and a cooler, comparatively drier season lasts through January. From February through April, the country is hot and dry. Temperatures in Vientiane normally range between 57° F. (13.8° C) and 93° F. (33.8° C) during the year. Humidity is high most of the year.

Greatest Distances: Northwest to southeast: 650 mi. (1,046 km)
Northeast to southwest: 315 mi. (510 km)

Area: 91,431 sq. mi. (236,804 km²)

NATURE

Trees: Laos has tropical rain forests of broadleaf evergreens in the north (oak, pine, magnolia, and laurel) and monsoon forests in the south of mixed evergreens and deciduous trees (teak, rosewood, ebony, and sandalwood). The ground in the monsoon areas is covered with a tall, coarse grass called *tranh*, and an abundance of bamboo, scrub, and wild banana trees. Forests cover two-thirds of Laos.

Animals: Animal life includes tigers, elephants, leopards, panthers, lizards, cobras, crocodiles, and water buffalo, as well as bears, deer, rabbits, and squirrels.

Fish: Carp, catfish, mullet, and perch are found in the rivers and lakes of this landlocked country.

EVERYDAY LIFE

Food: Rice constitutes approximately 90 percent of the daily diet. Other mainstays are fish, eggs, chicken, pork, and only rarely a bit of beef, together with fruits and vegetables. Rice is served with chiles and a spicy paste made from fermented fish. A thick soup of meat or fish sometimes is served with rice. Hot chicken soup often is seasoned with a paste of pounded onions, garlic, and stinging red peppers.

Housing: For most of the population housing is simple. Materials come from the neighboring forest, and the labor is provided by the householder, his family, and possibly a neighbor. The typical house is rectangular, built on long poles rising to and supporting the roof. Roofs are usually thatched.

Houses for people with higher living standards are larger and customarily of wooden construction, but usually retain the thatch roofing.

In towns stucco is common but brick is becoming increasingly popular. Merchants make their homes above their shops. Only in urban areas are dwellings electrified.

Holidays: Many festivals are related to the cycle of rice cultivation, and they are observed in rural areas where holidays celebrated on specific calendar dates are not well understood. There also are fifteen religious festivals celebrated each year.

The following holidays are observed in larger villages and towns:

> March 24, Army Day
> April 14-16, Lao New Year (Water Festival)
> May, Boum Bam Fay, a celebration of Buddha's birth, enlightenment, and death
> May 11, Constitution Day
> July 19, Laos Independence Day, celebrating the treaty of 1949 in which Laos became a sovereign state within the French union
> December 24, Sovereignty Day, celebrating the achievement of autonomy in 1954

Culture: Probably the best-known form of Lao art is the architecture, ornamentation, and sculpture of the Buddhist pagodas called wats. Small Buddhas carved of ivory and wood also are worn around the neck or grace the home. Larger Buddhas may be as large as 18 ft. (5 m) tall.

Laotian literature is predominantly religious and is linked to the Buddhist tradition. It is generally enclosed in the temple libraries. There is also a secular literary stream based on themes of Hindu epic poems, which have been transmuted into popular language. The best-known existing history is the *Nithane Khun Borom*.

Folk arts include silver work and gold work, ivory and wood carving, basket making, and weaving. Musical themes are closely related to religion. Music is not written down but is played from memory. Dance troupes draw upon themes from Indian epics. All professional dancers are male.

Sports and Recreation: Song, story, and play are important leisure-time activities in Laos. Soccer games are organized as competitions between towns or between teams picked randomly on a village field. Volleyball is popular also.

Communication: Communication is extremely primitive. The government controls the communications media. There are two daily newspapers, 225,000 radio receivers, 30,000 television sets, and 4,300 telephones.

Transportation: A railroad linking Vietnam and Laos has been under construction. During French rule, a primitive system of roads was created, but only one-third of the roads are paved, and half are unusable in rainy season. There are 7 airports; the Wattay international airport at Vientiane connects with Bangkok, Thailand; Phnom Penh, Kampuchea; and Hong Kong.

Rivers are major avenues of transport, though natural obstacles limit navigation considerably.

Education: Classes conducted by Buddhist monks are all that are available in some villages. The literacy rate remains low: 55 percent for males, 25 percent for females, but the government has set up a number of literacy programs in provincial villages. The Communist government now requires that classes from elementary through university levels be taught in Lao.

The educational system includes five-year primary schools, six-year secondary schools, technical schools, teacher-training schools, and one university. There also are schools for law and public administration and for medicine. The government has set up a number of agricultural schools as well.

Health: Health conditions are poor. Extension of services to rural areas has been a high priority of the government. Trained personnel are in short supply, but their number is slowly increasing.

Malaria and gastroenteritis are the major health problems, and malnutrition is widespread.

ECONOMY AND INDUSTRY

Agriculture: Cardamom, citrus fruits, corn, rice, tea, tobacco, cotton, coffee, cattle, opium
Forest products: Benzoin, teak
Principal Products: Tin, leather goods, pottery, silk, silver work

IMPORTANT DATES

A.D. 700 — Lao Lum migrate to Laos

1353 — What is now Laos is united into kingdom of Lan Xang (land of a million elephants)

1717—Three separate kingdoms—Luang Prabang, Vientiane, and Champassak—are formed

18th century—Rulers of three Laotian kingdoms become vassals of Siam

1800s—Ancestors of the Lao and Tai move into Laos

1907—France makes Laos a protectorate

1945—Japanese drive French from Indochina and declare the independence of Laos

1947—A Free Laos committee, headed by brother princes Phetsarath, Souvanna Phouma, and Souphanouvong, negotiates Laos's first constitution with France

1949—Independence within the French Union is achieved

1950—Captain Kong Le, a Laotian army officer, overthrows pro-Western government and demands neutralist government

1954—Ho Chi Minh (North Korean Communist leader) defeats French at Dien Bien Phu in Vietnam. Laos is established as buffer state between North Vietnam and Thailand

1955—Laos becomes a member of the UN

1956—Laos at edge of civil war

1961—Cease-fire ends civil war

1962—Fourteen-nation conference at Geneva sets up coalition government in Laos

1963—Fighting breaks out again between the Pathet Lao (the Communist rebel movement) and government forces; Pathet Lao receives support from Chinese, Soviet, and North Vietnamese troops

1970—Souvanna Phouma's government troops control western Laos; Pathet Lao forces hold eastern Laos

1973—Provisional Government of National Unity is formed

1975—Pathet Lao takes control and establishes the Lao People's Democratic Republic

Early 1980s—Laos becomes junior partner in Vietnamese-led Indochina grouping of Laos, Vietnam, and Cambodia

1985—Border clashes occur between Laos and Thailand; Laos agrees to help U.S. search for U.S. servicemen lost during Indochina War

IMPORTANT PEOPLE

Prince Boun Oum, rightest leader; delegate to the 1962 Geneva Conference

Admiral Jean Decoux, governor-general under French administration cooperated with Japan during World War II

King Deo Van Tri (c. 1849-1908), avenged the Thais for his brothers' kidnapping; made agreement with France

Fa Ngum (1316-1373), became 22nd king in 1353; created empire called *Lan Xang*; responsible for growth of Therevada Buddhism; most famous person in Lao history

Faydang Lobliayao, Hmong chieftain who fought against French; member of central committee headed by Kaysone Phomvihane during early days of independence

Kaysone Phomvihane, chairman of central committee in policy-making role after monarchy was overthrown in 1970s

King Khun Borom, legendary first Lao monarch

Kong Le, captain of Lao Theung hill tribes; overthrew government in 1960; offered premiership to Souvanna Phouma

Oun Hueun, son of Fa Ngum; succeeded him as ruler

Oun Kham (1811 or 1816-95), king of Luang Prabang in 1880s

Auguste Pavie (1847-1925), Frenchman who came to Laos in 1886; convinced French of Laos's value

Prince Phetsarath (1890-1960), known as the Iron Man; tried to unify Laos after World War II; anti-French, anti-American, and anti-Communist

Charles Rochet, Frenchman interested in fostering Laotian culture

King Savang Vatthana, last Laotian king; deposed by Kaysone Phomvihane

Sisomphone Louansay, a tribal Tai; member of central committee chaired by Kaysone Phomvihane in 1970s

King Souligna Vongsa, ruler when Europeans came in 1641; ruled for 57 years in era called Golden Age of Laos

Souphanouvong (1912-   ), called the Red Prince; half-brother of Phetsarath and Souvanna Phouma; leftist

Souvanna Phouma (1901-   ), neutralist; premier in 1951-54, 1956-58, 1960, 1962-64, 1965-75; advisor to Communist government, 1975

Tiao Anou, nineteenth-century Laotian ruler of Vientiane

Touby Lyfong (-1975), chief of Hmong people; minister of health in national government

Vang Pao, Hmong general who became part of pro-Western forces in the 1970s

125

INDEX

Page numbers that appear in boldface type indicate illustrations

About the Author

Judith Diamond is a writer and an educator who has worked in the Laotian community for a number of years. She was greatly helped in the preparation of this book by the Indochinese Refugee Center in Elgin, Illinois, and the Lao Association in Chicago. The following people especially gave much of their time: Somlith Vixaysouk, Seng Angpraseuth, Souk Vongsaga, and Kris Abhay.